Fremdsprachentexte

Nadine Gordimer
Town and Country Lovers

Three Stories

Herausgegeben von
Helmut Winter

Philipp Reclam jun. Stuttgart

Diese Ausgabe darf nur in der Bundesrepublik Deutschland, in Österreich und in der Schweiz vertrieben werden.

Universal-Bibliothek Nr. 9237

Gesamtherstellung: Reclam, Ditzingen. Printed in Germany 2001
RECLAM und UNIVERSAL-BIBLIOTHEK sind eingetragene Marken der Philipp Reclam jun. GmbH & Co., Stuttgart
ISBN 3-15-009237-X

www.reclam.de

Some Monday For Sure

My sister's husband, Josias, used to work on the railways but then he got this job where they make dynamite for the mines. He was the one who sits out on that little iron seat clamped to the back of the big red truck, with a red flag in his hand. The idea is that if you drive up too near the truck or look as if you're going to crash into it, he waves the flag to warn you off. You've seen those trucks often on the Main Reef Road between Johannesburg and the mining towns – they carry the stuff and have DANGER – EXPLOSIVES painted on them. The man sits there, with an iron chain looped across his little seat to keep him from being thrown into the road, and he clutches his flag like a kid with a balloon. That's how Josias was, too. Of course, if you didn't take any notice of the warning and went on and crashed into the truck, he would be the first to be blown to high heaven and hell, but he always just sits there, this chap, as if he has no idea when he was born or that he might not die in a bed an old man of eighty. As if the dust in his eyes and the racket of the truck are going to last for ever.

5 **to clamp:** verklammern.
truck: Lastwagen.
9 **reef:** Riff, Klippe.
12 **to loop:** schlingen.
13 **to clutch:** greifen, packen.
18 **chap:** Bursche, Kerl.
20 **racket:** Krach, Lärm.

My sister knew she had a good man but she never said anything about being afraid of this job. She only grumbled in winter, when he was stuck out there in the cold and used to get a cough (she's a nurse), and in summer when it rained all day and she said he would land up with rheumatism, crippled, and then who would give him work? The dynamite people? I don't think it ever came into her head that any day, every day, he could be blown up instead of coming home in the evening. Anyway, you wouldn't have thought so by the way she took it when he told us what it was he was going to have to do.

I was working down at a garage in town, that time, at the petrol pumps, and I was eating before he came in because I was on night shift. Emma had the water ready for him and he had a wash without saying much, as usual, but then he didn't speak when they sat down to eat, either, and when his fingers went into the mealie meal he seemed to forget what it was he was holding and not to be able to shape it into a mouthful. Emma must have thought he felt too dry to eat, because she got up and brought him a jam tin of the beer she had made for Saturday. He drank it and then sat back and looked from her to me, but she said, "Why don't you eat?" and he began to, slowly. She said, "What's the matter with you?" He got up and yawned and yawned, showing those brown chipped teeth that remind me of the big ape at the Johannesburg zoo that I saw once when I went with the

2f. **to grumble:** brummen, klagen, murren.
8f. **to blow up:** in die Luft sprengen.
12 **garage:** Tankstelle; Reparaturwerkstatt.
13 **petrol pump:** (Benzin-)Zapfsäule.
17 **mealie** (S.Afr.): Mais.
26 **to chip:** abbröckeln.

school. He went into the other room of the house, where he and Emma slept, and he came back with his pipe. He filled it carefully, the way a poor man does; I saw, as soon as I went to work at the filling station, how the white men fill their pipes, stuffing the tobacco in, picking out any bits they don't like the look of, shoving the tin half-shut back into the glove-box on the car. "I'm going down to Sela's place," said Emma. "I can go with Willie on his way to work if you don't want to come."

"No. Not tonight. You stay here." Josias always speaks like this, the short words of a schoolmaster or a boss-boy, but if you hear the way he says them, you know he is not really ordering you around at all, he is only asking you.

"No, I told her I'm coming," Emma said, in the voice of a woman having her own way in a little thing.

"Tomorrow." Josias began to yawn again, looking at us with wet eyes. "Go to bed," Emma said. "I won't be late."

"No, no, I want to . . ." He blew a sigh. "When he's gone, man –" He moved his pipe at me. "I'll tell you later."

Emma laughed. "What can you tell me that Willie can't hear." I've lived with them ever since they were married. Emma always was the one who looked after me, even before, when I was a little kid. It was true that whatever happened to us happened to us together. He looked at me; I suppose he saw that I was a man, now: I was in my blue overalls with *Shell* on the pocket and everything.

4 **filling station:** Tankstelle.
6 **to shove:** schieben, stoßen.
7 **glove-box:** Handschuhfach.
11 **boss-boy:** Chefdiener.
13 **to order s.o. around:** jdn. herumkommandieren.
27 **overalls** (pl.): Arbeitskittel, -hose.

He said, “They want me to do something . . . a job with the truck.”

Josias used to turn out regularly to political meetings and he took part in a few protests before everything went underground, but he had never been more than one of the crowd. We had Mandela and the rest of the leaders, cut out of the paper, hanging on the wall, but he had never known, personally, any of them. Of course there were his friends Ndhlovu and Seb Masinde who said they had gone underground and who occasionally came late at night for a meal or slept in my bed for a few hours.

“They want to stop the truck on the road –”

“Stop it?” Emma was like somebody stepping into cold dark water; with every word that was said she went deeper. “But how can you do it – when? Where will they do it?” She was wild, as if she must go out and prevent it all happening right then.

I felt that cold water of Emma’s rising round the belly because Emma and I often had the same feelings, but I caught also, in Josias’s not looking at me, a signal Emma couldn’t know. Something in me jumped at it like catching a swinging rope. “They want the stuff inside . . . ?”

Nobody said anything.

I said, “What a lot of big bangs you could make with that, man,” and then shut up before Josias needed to tell me to.

“So what’re you going to do?” Emma’s mouth stayed open after she had spoken, the lips pulled back.

3 **to turn out to s.th.:** zu etas ausrücken, an etwas teilnehmen.

6 **Mandela:** Nelson Rolihlahia M. (geb. 1918) südafrikanischer Politiker und Bürgerrechtler.

18 **belly:** Bauch, Leib.

"They'll tell me everything. I just have to give them the best place on the road – that'll be the Free State road, the others're too busy ... and ... the time when we pass ..."

"You'll be dead." Emma's head was shuddering and her whole body shook; I've never seen anybody give up like that. He was dead already, she saw it with her eyes and she was kicking and screaming without knowing how to show it to him. She looked like she wanted to kill Josias herself, for being dead. "That'll be the finish, for sure. He's got a gun, the white man in front, hasn't he, you told me. And the one with him? They'll kill you. You'll go to prison. They'll take you to Pretoria jail and hang you by the rope ... Yes, he's got the gun, you told me, didn't you – many times you told me –"

"The others've got guns too. How d'you think they can hold us up? They've got guns and they'll come all round him. It's all worked out –"

"The one in front will shoot you, I know it, don't tell me, I know what I say ..." Emma went up and down and around till I thought she would push the walls down – they wouldn't have needed much pushing, in that house in Alexandra Township – and I was scared of her. I don't mean for what she would do to me if I got in her way, or to Josias, but for what might happen to her: something like taking a fit or screaming that none of us would be able to forget.

I don't think Josias was sure about doing the job before but he wanted to do it now. "No shooting. Nobody will

23 **township:** von der südafrikanischen Regierung angelegte Siedlung mit Unterkünften für Schwarze.

26 **fit:** Anfall, Anwandlung.

shoot me. Nobody will know that I know anything. Nobody will tell them anything. I'm held up just the same like the others! Same as the white man in front! Who can shoot me? They can shoot me for that?"

"Someone else can go, I don't want it, do you hear? You will stay at home, I will say you are sick . . . You will be killed, they will shoot you . . . Josias, I'm telling you, I don't want . . . I won't . . ."

I was waiting my chance to speak, all the time, and I felt Josias was waiting to talk to someone who had caught the signal. I said quickly, while she went on and on, "But even on the road there are some cars?"

"Roadblocks," he said, looking at the floor. "They've got the signs, the ones you see when a road's being dug up, and there'll be some men with picks. After the truck goes through they'll block the road so that any other cars turn off onto the old road there by Kalmansdrif. The same thing on the other side, two miles on. There where the farm road goes down to Nek Halt."

"Hell, man! Did you have to pick that part of the road?"

"I know it like this yard. Don't I?"

Emma stood there, between the two of us, while we discussed the whole business. We didn't have to worry about anyone hearing, not only because Emma kept the window wired up in that kitchen, but also because the yard the house was in was a real Alexandra Township one, full of babies yelling and people shouting, night and day, not to mention the transistors playing in the houses

13 **roadblock:** Straßensperre.
15 **pick:** Spitzhacke.
20 **to pick:** aussuchen.
25 **to wire up:** mit Draht bespannen.
27 **to yell:** schreien.

all round. Emma was looking at us all the time and out of the corner of my eye I could see her big front going up and down fast in the neck of her dress.

"... so they're going to tie you up as well as the others?"

He drew on his pipe to answer me.

We thought for a moment and then grinned at each other; it was the first time for Josias, that whole evening.

Emma began collecting the dishes under our noses. She dragged the tin bath of hot water from the stove and washed up. "I said I'm taking my day off on Wednesday. I suppose this is going to be next week." Suddenly, yet talking as if carrying on where she let up, she was quite different.

"I don't know."

"Well, I have to know because I suppose I must be at home."

"What must you be at home for?" said Josias.

"If the police come I don't want them talking to *him*," she said, looking at us both without wanting to see us.

"The police –" said Josias, and jerked his head to send them running, while I laughed, to show her.

"And I want to know what I must say."

"What must you say? Why? They can get my statement from me when they find us tied up. In the night I'll be back here myself."

"Oh yes," she said, scraping the mealie meal he hadn't

4 **to tie up:** zusammenbinden.
12 **day off:** freier Tag.
22 **to jerk:** ruckartig bewegen.
28 **to scrape:** kratzen.

eaten back into the pot. She did everything as usual; she wanted to show us nothing was going to wait because of this big thing, she must wash the dishes and put ash on the fire. "You'll be back, oh yes. – Are you going to sit here all night, Willie? – Oh yes, you'll be back."
And then, I think, for a moment Josias saw himself dead, too; he didn't answer when I took my cap and said, so long, from the door.

I knew it must be a Monday. I notice that women quite often don't remember ordinary things like this, I don't know what they think about – for instance, Emma didn't catch on that it must be Monday, next Monday or the one after, some Monday for sure, because Monday was the day that we knew Josias went with the truck to the Free State mines. It was Friday when he told us and all day Saturday I had a terrible feeling that it was going to be *that* Monday, and it would be all over before I could – what? I didn't know, man. I felt I must at least see where it was going to happen. Sunday I was off work and I took my bicycle and rode into town before there was even anybody in the streets and went to the big station and found that although there wasn't a train on Sundays that would take me all the way, I could get one that would take me about thirty miles. I had to pay to put the bike in the luggage van as well as for my ticket, but I'd got my wages on Friday. I got off at the nearest halt to Kalmansdrif and then I asked people along the road the best way. It was a long ride, more than two hours. I came out on the

19 **to be off work:** einen arbeitsfreien Tag haben.
25 **luggage van:** Gepäckwagen.

main raod from the sand road just at the turn-off Josias had told me about. It was just like he said: a tin sign KALMANSDRIF pointing down the road I'd come from. And the nice blue tarred road, smooth, straight ahead: was I glad to get on to it! I hadn't taken much notice of the country so far, while I was sweating along, but from then on I woke up and saw everything. I've only got to think about it to see it again now. The veld is flat round about there, it was the end of winter, so the grass was dry. Quite far away and very far apart, there was a hill and then another, sticking up in the middle of nothing, pink colour, and with its point cut off like the neck of a bottle. Ride and ride, these hills never got any nearer and there were none beside the road. It all looked empty and the sky much bigger than the ground, but there were some people there. It's funny you don't notice them like you do in town. All our people, of course; there were barbed-wire fences, so it must have been white farmers' land, but they've got the water and their houses are far off the road and you can usually see them only by the big dark trees that hide them. Our people had mud houses and there would be three or four in the same place made bare by goats and people's feet. Often the huts were near a kind of crack in the ground, where the little kids played and where, I suppose, in summer, there was water. Even now the women were managing to do washing in some places. I saw children run to the road to jig about and stamp

1 **turn-off:** Abzweigung.
4 **to tar:** teeren, asphaltieren.
8 **veld:** offenes Grasland in Südafrika.
17 f. **barbed-wire fence:** Stacheldrahtzaun.
24 **crack:** Riß, Sprung.
27 **to jig about:** herumtanzen.

when cars passed, but the men and women took no interest in what was up there. It was funny to think that I was just like them, now, men and women who are always busy inside themselves with jobs, plans, thinking about how to get money or how to talk to someone about something important, instead of like the children, as I used to be only a few years ago, taking in each small thing around them as it happens.

Still, there were people living pretty near the road. What would they do if they saw the dynamite truck held up and a fight going on? (I couldn't think of it, then, in any other way except like I'd seen hold-ups in Western, although I've seen plenty of fighting, all my life, among the Location gangs and drunks – I was ashamed not to be able to forget those kid-stuff Westerns at a time like this.) Would they go running away to the white farmer? Would somebody jump on a bike and go for the police? Or if there was no bike, what about a horse? I saw someone riding a horse.

I rode slowly to the next turn-off, the one where a farm road goes down to Nek Halt. There it was, just like Josias said. Here was where the other roadblock would be. But when he spoke about it there was nothing inbetween! No people, no houses, no flat veld with hills on it! It had been just one of those things grown-ups see worked out in their heads: while all the time, here it was, a real place where people had cooking fires, I could hear a herdboy yelling at a dirty bundle of sheep, a big bird I've never

12 **hold-up:** Raubüberfall.
13 f. **location:** Siedlung für Schwarze, meist in der Nähe einer Kleinstadt.
14 **gang:** Bande, Horde.
15 **kid-stuff:** für Kinder geeignet.

seen in town balanced on the barbed-wire fence right in front of me ... I got off my bike and it flew away.

I sat a minute on the side of the road. I'd had a cold drink in an Indian shop in the dorp where I'd got off the train, but I was dry again inside my mouth, while plenty of water came out of my skin, I can tell you. I rode back down the road looking for the exact place I would choose if I was Josias. There was a stretch where there was only one kraal with two houses, and that quite a way back from the road. Also there was a dip where the road went over a donga. Old stumps of trees and nothing but cows' business down there; men could hide. I got off again and had a good look round.

But I wondered about the people, up top. I don't know why it was, I wanted to know about those people just as though I was going to have to go and live with them or something. I left the bike down in the donga and crossed the road behind a Cadillac going so fast the air smacked together after it, and I began to trek over the veld to the houses. I know most of our people live like this, in the veld, but I'd never been into houses like that before. I was born in some Location (I don't know which one, I must ask Emma one day) and Emma and I lived in Moroka with our grandmother. Our mother worked in town and she used to come and see us sometimes, but we never saw our father and Emma thinks perhaps we didn't have the same father, because she remembers a man

4 **dorp** (Afrik.): Dorf, kleine Stadt.
9 **kraal:** Umzäunung, Ansiedlung; Hüttendorf in Südafrika.
10 **dip:** Senkung.
11 **donga** (S. Afr.): (durch Erosion entstandener) tiefer Graben.
18 **to smack:** knallen, klatschen.
19 **to trek:** eine beschwerliche Reise machen.

before I was born, and after I was born she didn't see him again. I don't really remember anyone, from when I was a little kid, except Emma. Emma dragging me along so fast my arm almost came off my body, because we had nearly been caught by the Indian while stealing peaches from his lorry: we did that every day.
We lived in one room with our grandmother but it was a tin house with a number and later on there was a street-light at the corner. These houses I was coming to had a pattern all over them marked into the mud they were built of. There was a mound of dried cows' business, as tall as I was, stacked up in a pattern, too. And then the usual junk our people have, just like in the Location: old tins, broken things collected from white people's rubbish heaps. The fowls ran sideways from my feet and two old men let their talking die away into ahas and ehês as I came up. I greeted them the right way to greet old men and they nodded and went on ehêing and ahaing to show that they had been greeted properly. One of them had very clean ragged trousers tied with string and he sat on the ground, but the other, sitting on a bucket-seat that must have been taken from some scrapyard car, was dressed in a way I've never seen – from the old days, I suppose. He wore a black suit with very wide trousers, laced boots, a stiff white collar and black tie, and on top

11 **mound:** Erdwall.
12 **to stack:** aufschichten.
13 **junk:** Trödel, Gerümpel.
14 f. **rubbish heap:** Müllhaufen.
15 **fowl:** Geflügel, Hühner.
16 **to die away:** schwächer werden, verhallen.
20 **ragged:** zerlumpt.
22 **scrapyard:** Schrottplatz.

of it all, a broken old hat. It was Sunday, of course, so I suppose he was all dressed up. I've heard that these people who work for farmers wear sacks most of the time. The old ones didn't ask me what I wanted there. They just peered at me with their eyes gone the colour of soapy water because they were so old. And I didn't know what to say because I hadn't thought what I was going to say, I'd just walked. Then a little kid slipped out of the dark doorway quick as a cockroach. I thought perhaps everyone else was out because it was Sunday but then a voice called from inside the other house, and when the child didn't answer, called again, and a woman came to the doorway.

I said my bicycle had a puncture and could I have some water.

She said something into the house and in a minute a girl, about fifteen she must've been, edged past her carrying a paraffin tin and went off to fetch water. Like all the girls that age, she never looked at you. Her body shook under an ugly old dress and she almost hobbled in her hurry to get away. Her head was tied up in a rag-doek right down to the eyes the way old-fashioned people do, otherwise she would have been quite pretty, like any other girl. When she had gone a little way the kid went pumping after her, panting, yelling, opening his skinny legs wide

5 **to peer:** anstarren, spähen, gucken.
9 **cockroach:** Küchenschabe.
14 **puncture:** Reifenpanne.
20 **to hobble:** humpeln, hinken.
21 **rag-doek:** Lumpentuch (von afrikanischen Frauen zum Verhüllen des Kopfes getragen) (*doek* [Afrik.]: Tuch).
25 **to pant:** keuchen.

as scissors over stones and antheaps, and then he caught up with her and you could see that right away she was quite different, I knew how it was, she yelled at him, you heard her laughter as she chased him with the tin, whirled around from out of his clutching hands, struggled with him; they were together like Emma and I used to be when we got away from the old lady, and from the school, and everybody. And Emma was also one of our girls who have the big strong comfortable bodies of mothers even when they're still kids, maybe it comes from always lugging the smaller one round on their backs.

A man came out of the house behind the woman and was friendly. His hair had the dusty look of someone who's been sleeping off drink. In fact, he was still a bit heavy with it.

"You coming from Jo'burg?"

But I wasn't going to be caught out being careless at all, Josias could count on me for that.

"Vereeniging."

He thought there was something funny there – nobody dresses like a Jo'burger, you could always spot us a mile off – but he was too full to follow it up.

He stood stretching his sticky eyelids open and then he fastened on me the way some people will do: "Can't you get me work there where you are?"

"What kind of work?"

He waved a hand describing me. "You got a good work."

1 **antheap:** Ameisenhaufen.
10 **to lug:** schleppen.
19 **Vereeniging:** Stadt in Südafrika.
21 **to spot:** bemerken, erkennen.

"'Sall right."

"Where you working now?"

"Garden boy."

He tittered, "Look like you work in town," shook his head.

I was surprised to find the woman handing me a tin of beer, and I squatted on the ground to drink it. It's mad to say that a mud house can be pretty, but those patterns made in the mud looked nice. They must have been done with a sharp stone or stick when the mud was smooth and wet, the shapes of things like big leaves and moons filled in with lines that went all one way in this shape, another way in that, so that as you looked at the walls in the sun, some shapes were dark and some were light, and if you moved the light ones went dark and the dark ones got light instead. The girl came back with the heavy tin of water on her head making her neck thick. I washed out the jam tin I'd had the beer in and filled it with water. When I thanked them, the old men stirred and ahead and ehêd again. The man made as if to walk bit with me, but I was lucky, he didn't go more than a few yards. "No good," he said. "Every morning, five o'clock, and the pay – very small."

How I would have hated to be him, a man already married and with big children, working all his life in the fields wearing sacks. When you think like this about someone he seems something you could never possibly be, as if it's his fault, and not just the chance of where he happened to be born. At the same time I had a crazy feeling I wanted to tell him something wonderful, something he'd never

4 **to titter:** kichern.
7 **to squat:** kauern, hocken.

dreamed could happen, something he'd fall on his knees and thank me for. I wanted to say, "Soon you'll be the farmer yourself and you'll have shoes like me and your girl will get water from your windmill. Because on Monday, or another Monday, the truck will stop down there and all the stuff will be taken away and they – Josias, me; even you, yes – we'll win for ever." But instead all I said was, "Who did that on your house?" He didn't understand and I made a drawing in the air with my hand. "The women," he said, not interested.

Down in the donga I sat a while and then threw away the tin and rode off without looking up again to where the kraal was.

It wasn't that Monday. Emma and Josias go to bed very early and of course they were asleep by the time I got home late on Sunday night – Emma thought I'd been with the boys I used to go around with at weekends. But Josias got up at half past four every morning, then, because it was a long way from the Location to where the dynamite factory was, and although I didn't usually even hear him making the fire in the kitchen which was also where I was sleeping, that morning I was awake the moment he got out of bed next door. When he came into the kitchen I was sitting up in my blankets and I whispered loudly, "I went there yesterday. I saw the turn-off and everything. Down there by the donga, ay? Is that the place?"

He looked at me, a bit dazed. He nodded. Then: "Wha'd' you mean you went there?"

"I could see that's the only good place. I went up to the

28 **to daze:** betäuben, verwirren, blenden.

house, too, just to see ... the people are all right. Not many. When it's not Sunday there may be nobody there but the old man – there were two, I think one was just a visitor. The man and the women will be over in the fields somewhere, and that must be quite far, because you can't see the mealies from the road ..." I could feel myself being listened to carefully, getting in with him (and if with him, with *them*) while I was talking, and I knew exactly what I was saying, absolutely clearly, just as I would know exactly what I was doing. He began to question me; but like I was an older man or a clever one; he didn't know what to say. He drank his tea while I told him all about it. He was thinking. Just before he left he said, "I shouldn't've told you."

I ran after him, outside, into the yard. It was still dark. I blurted in the same whisper we'd been using, "Not today, is it?" I couldn't see his face properly but I knew he didn't know whether to answer or not. "Not today." I was so happy I couldn't go to sleep again.

In the evening Josias managed to make some excuse to come out with me alone for a bit. He said, "I told them you were a hundred-per-cent. It's just the same as if I know." "Of course, no difference. I just haven't had much of a chance to do anything ..." I didn't carry on: "... because I was too young"; we didn't want to bring Emma into it. And anyway, no one but a real kid is too young any more. Look at the boys who are up for sabotage. I said, "Have they got them all?"

He hunched his shoulders.

16 **to blurt:** (mit etwas) herausplatzen.

29 **to hunch one's shoulders:** die Schultern hochziehen, einen Buckel machen.

"I mean, even the ones for the picks and spades . . .?" He wouldn't say anything, but I knew I could ask. "Oh, boetie, man, even just to keep a lookout, there on the road . . ."

I know he didn't want it but once they knew I knew, and that I'd been there and everything, they were keen to use me. At least that's what I think. I never went to any meetings or anything where it was planned, and beforehand I only met the two others who were with me at the turn-off in the end, and we were told exactly what we had to do by Seb Masinde. Of course, Josias and I never said a word to Emma. The Monday that we did it was three weeks later and I can tell you, although a lot's happened to me since then, I'll never forget the moment when we flagged the truck through with Josias sitting there on the back in his little seat. Josias! I wanted to laugh and shout there in the veld; I didn't feel scared – what was there to be scared of, he'd been sitting on a load of dynamite every day of his life for years now, so what's the odds. We had one of those tins of fire and a bucket of tar and the real ROAD CLOSED signs from the P. W. D. and everything went smooth at our end. It was at the Nek Halt end that the trouble started when one of these A.A. patrol bikes had to come along (Josias says it was some-

1 **spade:** Spaten.
3 **boetie** (Afrik.): Freund.
15 **to flag through:** mit einer Fahne (durch)winken.
19f. **what's the odds:** etwa: was macht das schon, was ist Besonderes daran.
21 **tar:** Teer.
P. W. D.: Abk. für Pretoria-Witwatersrand-District.
23 **A. A.:** Abk. für Automobile Association.
24 **patrol:** Patrouille, Kontrolle.

thing new, they'd never met a patrol on that road that time of day, before) and get suspicious about the block there. In the meantime the truck was stopped all right but someone was shot and Josias tried to get the gun from the white man up in front of the truck and there was a hell of a fight and they had to make a getaway with the stuff in a car and van back through our block, instead of taking over the truck and driving it to a hiding place to offload. More than half the stuff had to be left behind in the truck. Still, they got clean away with what they did get and it was never found by the police. Whenever I read in the papers here that something's been blown up back at home, I wonder if it's still one of our bangs. Two of our people got picked up right away and some more later and the whole thing was all over the papers with speeches by the chief of Special Branch about a master plot and everything. But Josias got away okay. We three chaps at the road block just ran into the veld to where there were bikes hidden. We went to a place we'd been told in Rustenburg district for a week and then we were told to get over to Bechuanaland. It wasn't so bad; we had no money but around Rustenburg it was easy to pinch pawpaws and oranges off the farms ... Oh, I sent a message to Emma that I was all right; and at that time it didn't seem true that I couldn't go home again.

But in Bechuanaland it was different. We had no money, and you don't find food on trees in that dry place. They said they would send us money; it didn't come. But Josias

8 **to offload:** abladen.
16 **Special Branch:** Sicherheitspolizei.
22 **to pinch:** klauen, stehlen.
22 f. **pawpaw:** Papaya-Frucht.

was there too, and we stuck together; people hid us and we kept going. Planes arrived and took away the big shots and the white refugees but although we were told we'd go too, it never came off. We had no money to pay for ourselves. There were plenty others like us in the beginning. At last we just walked, right up Bechuanaland and through Northern Rhodesia to Mbeya, that's over the border in Tanganyika, where we were headed for. A long walk; took Josias and me months. We met up with a chap who'd been given a bit of money and from there sometimes we went by bus. No one asks questions when you're nobody special and you walk, like all the other African people themselves, or take the buses, that the whites never use; it's only if you've got the money for cars or to arrive at the airports that all these things happen that you read about: getting sent back over the border, refused permits and so on. So we got here, to Tanganyika at last, down to this town of Dar es Salaam where we'd been told we'd be going.

There's a refugee camp here and they give you a shilling or two a day until you get work. But it's out of town, for one thing, and we soon left there and found a room down in the shanty town. There are some nice buildings, of course, in the real town – nothing like Johannesburg or Durban, though – and that used to be the white town, the whites who are left still live there, but the Africans with big jobs in the government and so on live there too. Some of our leaders who are refugees like us live in these

2f. **the big shots:** die ‚hohen Tiere'.
3 **refugee:** Flüchtling.
18 **Dar es Salaam:** Hauptstadt von Tansania (von arab. *Dar es Salaam* ›Ort des Friedens‹).
23 **shanty town:** Slum(vor)stadt mit Elendsquartieren.

houses and have big cars; everyone knows they're important men, here, not like at home where if you're black you're just rubbish for the Locations. The people down where we lived are very poor and it's hard to get work because they haven't got enough work for themselves, but I've got my Standard Seven and I managed to get a small job as a clerk. Josias never found steady work. But that didn't matter so much because the big thing was that Emma was able to come to join us after five months, and she and I earn the money. She's a nurse, you see, and Africanization started in the hospitals and the government was short of nurses. So Emma got the chance to come up with a party of them sent for specially from South Africa and Rhodesia. We were very lucky because it's impossible for people to get their families up here. She came in a plane paid for by the government, and she and the other girls had their photograph taken for the newspaper as they got off at the airport. That day she came we took her to the beach, where everyone can bathe, no restrictions, and for a cool drink in one of the hotels (she'd never been in a hotel before), and we walked up and down the road along the bay where everyone walks and where you can see the ships coming in and going out so near that the men out there wave to you. Whenever we bumped into anyone else from home they would stop and ask her about home, and how everything was. Josias and I couldn't stop grinning to hear us all, in the middle of Dar, talking away in our language about the things we know. That day it was like it had happened

6 **Standard Seven:** viertes Jahr in der südafrikanischen High School.
20 **restriction:** Einschränkung.
25 **to bump into s.o.:** jdn. zufällig treffen.

already: the time when we are home again and everything is our way.

Well, that's nearly three years ago, since Emma came. Josias has been sent away now and there's only Emma and me. That was always the idea, to send us away for training. Some go to Ethiopia and some go to Algeria and all over the show and by the time they come back there won't be anything Verwoerd's men know in the way of handling guns and so on that they won't know better. That's for a start. I'm supposed to go too, but some of us have been waiting a long time. In the meantime I go to work and I walk about this place in the evenings and I buy myself a glass of beer in a bar when I've got money. Emma and I have still got the flat we had before Josias left and two nurses from the hospital pay us for the other bedroom. Emma still works at the hospital but I don't know how much longer. Most days now since Josias's gone she wants me to walk up to fetch her from the hospital when she comes off duty, and when I get under the trees on the drive I see her staring out looking for me as if I'll never turn up ever again. Every day it's like that. When I come up she smiles and looks like she used to for a minute but by the time we're ten yards on the road she's shaking and shaking her head until the tears come, and saying over and over, "A person can't stand it, a person can't stand it." She said right from the beginning that the hospitals here are not like the hospitals at home, where the nurses have to know their job.

8 **Verwoerd:** Hendrik Frensch V. (1901–66), südafrikanischer Politiker, ab 1958 Ministerpräsident; entschiedener Verfechter der 1948 verkündeten Apartheids-Doktrin.

She's got a whole ward in her charge and now she says they're worse and worse and she can't trust anyone to do anything for her. And the staff don't like having strangers working with them anyway. She tells me every day like she's telling me for the first time. Of course it's true that some of the people don't like us being here. You know how it is, people haven't got enough jobs to go round, themselves. But I don't take much notice; I'll be sent off one of these days and until then I've got to eat and that's that.

The flat is nice with a real bathroom and we are paying off the table and six chairs she liked so much, but when we walk in, her face is terrible. She keeps saying the place will never be straight. At home there was only a tap in the yard for all the houses but she never said it there. She doesn't sit down for more than a minute without getting up at once again, but you can't get her to go out, even on these evenings when it's so hot you can't breathe. I go down to the market to buy the food now, she says she can't stand it. When I asked why – because at the beginning she used to like the market, where you can pick a live fowl for yourself, quite cheap – she said those little rotten tomatoes they grow here, and dirty people all shouting and she can't understand. She doesn't sleep, half the time, at night, either, and lately she wakes me up. It happened only last night. She was standing there in the dark and she said, "I felt bad." I said, "I'll make you some tea," though what good could tea do. "There must be something the matter with me," she says. "I must go to the doctor tomorrow."

1 **ward:** Abteilung, (Krankenhaus-)Station.
charge: Leitung, Verantwortung.

"Is it pains again, or what?"

She shakes her head slowly, over and over, and I know she's going to cry again. "A place where there's no one. I get up and look out the window and it's just like I'm not awake. And every day, every day. I can't ever wake up and be out of it. I always see this town."

Of course it's hard for her. I've picked up Swahili and I can get around all right; I mean I can always talk to anyone if I feel like it, but she hasn't learnt more than *ahsante* – she could've picked it up just as easily, but she *can't*, if you know what I mean. It's just a noise to her, like dogs barking or those black crows in the palm trees. When anyone does come here to see her – someone else from home, usually, or perhaps I bring the Rhodesian who works where I do – she only sits there and whatever anyone talks about she doesn't listen until she can sigh and say, "Heavy, heavy. Yes, for a woman alone. No friends, nobody. For a woman alone, I can tell you."

Last night I said to her, "It would be worse if you were at home, you wouldn't have seen Josias or me for a long time."

But she said, "Yes, it would be bad. Sela and everybody. And the old crowd at the hospital – but just the same, it would be bad. D'you remember how we used to go right into Jo'burg on my Saturday off? The people – ay! Even when you were twelve you used to be scared you'd lose me."

"I wasn't scared, you were the one was scared to get run

7 **Swahili:** Suaheli (Bantusprache, heute Amtssprache in Tansania, Uganda und Kenia).
10 **ahsante** (Suaheli): danke.
12 **crow:** Krähe.

over sometimes." But in the Location when we stole fruit, and sweets from the shops, Emma could always grab me out of the way of trouble, Emma always saved me. The same Emma. And yet it's not the same. And what could I do for her?

I suppose she wants to be back there now. But still she wouldn't be the same. I don't often get the feeling she knows what I'm thinking about, any more, or that I know what she's thinking, but she said, "You and he go off, you come back or perhaps you don't come back, you know what you must do. But for a woman? What shall I do there in my life? What shall I do here? What time is this for a woman?"

It's hard for her. Emma. She'll say all that often now, I know. She tells me everything so many times. Well, I don't mind it when I fetch her from the hospital and I don't mind going to the market. But straight after we've eaten, now, in the evenings, I let her go through it once and then I'm off. To walk in the streets when it gets a bit cooler in the dark. I don't know why it is, but I'm thinking so bloody hard about getting out there in the streets that I push down my food as fast as I can without her noticing. I'm so keen to get going I feel queer, kind of tight and excited. Just until I can get out and not hear. I wouldn't even mind skipping the meal. In the streets in the evening everyone is out. On the grass along the bay the fat Indians in their white suits with their wives in those fancy coloured clothes. Men and their girls holding hands. Old watchmen like beggars, sleeping in the doorways of the shut shops. Up and down people walk, walk,

3 **to grab:** greifen, packen.
25 **to skip:** überspringen, auslassen.

just sliding one foot after the other because now and then, like somebody lifting a blanket, there's air from the sea. She should come out for a bit of air in the evening, man. It's an old, old place this, they say. Not the buildings, I mean; but the place. They say ships were coming here before even a place like London was a town. She thought the bay was so nice, that first day. The lights from the ships run all over the water and the palms show up a long time even after it gets dark. There's a smell I've smelled ever since we've been here – three years! I don't mean the smells in the shanty town; a special warm night-smell. You can even smell it at three in the morning. I've smelled it when I was standing about with Emma, by the window; it's as hot in the middle of the night here as it is in the middle of the day, at home – funny, when you look at the stars and the dark. Well, I'll be going off soon. It can't be long now. Now that Josias is gone. You've just got to wait your time; they haven't forgotten about you. Dar es Salaam. Dar. Sometimes I walk with another chap from home, he says some things, makes you laugh! He says the old watchmen who sleep in the doorways get their wives to come there with them. Well, I haven't seen it. He says we're definitely going with the next lot. Dar es Salaam. Dar. One day I suppose I'll remember it and tell my wife I stayed three years there, once. I walk and walk, along the bay, past the shops and hotels and the German church and the big bank, and through the mud streets between old shacks and stalls. It's dark there and full of other walking shapes as I wander past light coming from the cracks in the walls, where the people are in their homes.

28 **shack:** Hütte.

Which New Era Would That Be?

Jake Alexander, a big, fat coloured man, half Scottish, half African, was shaking a large pan of frying bacon on the gas stove in the back room of his Johannesburg printing shop when he became aware that someone was knocking on the door at the front of the shop. The sizzling fat and the voices of the five men in the back room with him almost blocked sounds from without, and the knocking was of the steady kind that might have been going on for quite a few minutes. He lifted the pan off the flame with one hand and with the other made an impatient silencing gesture, directed at the bacon as well as the voices. Interpreting the movement as one of caution, the men hurriedly picked up the tumblers and cups in which they had been taking their end-of-the-day brandy at their ease, and tossed the last of it down. Little yellow Klaas, whose hair was like ginger-coloured wire wool, stacked the cups and glasses swiftly and hid them behind the dirty curtain that covered a row of shelves.

"Who's that?" yelled Jake, wiping his greasy hands down his pants.

1 **era:** Ära, Zeitalter.
6f. **to sizzle:** brutzeln, brodeln.
14 **tumbler:** Becherglas.
16 **to toss down:** ‚hinunterkippen', rasch austrinken.
17 **ginger-coloured:** ingwerfarben.
18 **to stack:** aufstapeln.
20 **greasy:** fettig, klebrig, verschmiert.
21 **pants** (pl.): Hose.

There was a sharp and playful tattoo, followed by an English voice: "Me – Alister. For heaven's sake, Jake!"

The fat man put the pan back on the flame and tramped through the dark shop, past the idle presses, to the door, and flung it open. "Mr Halford!" he said. "Well, good to see you. Come in, man. In the back there, you can't hear a thing." A young Englishman with gentle eyes, a stern mouth and flat, colourless hair which grew in an untidy, confused spiral from a double crown, stepped back to allow a young woman to enter ahead of him. Before he could introduce her, she held out her hand to Jake, smiling, and shook his firmly. "Good evening. Jennifer Tetzel," she said.

"Jennifer, this is Jake Alexander," the young man managed to get in, over her shoulder.

The two had entered the building from the street through an archway lettered NEW ERA BUILDING. "Which new era would that be?" the young woman had wondered aloud, brightly, while they were waiting in the dim hallway for the door to be opened, and Alister Halford had not known whether the reference was to the discovery of deep-level gold mining that had saved Johannesburg from the ephemeral fate of a mining camp in the nineties, or to the optimism after the settlement of labour troubles in the twenties, or to the recovery after the world went off the gold standard in the thirties – really, one had no

1 **tattoo:** Zapfenstreich, Militärmusik.
4 **to tramp:** stapfen.
10 **crown:** Scheitel.
18 **archway:** Bogengang.
20 **hallway:** Korridor.
24 **ephemeral:** flüchtig, vorübergehend.

idea of the age of these buildings in this run-down end of the town. Now, coming in out of the deserted hallway gloom, which smelled of dust and rotting wood – the smell of waiting – they were met by the live, cold tang of ink and the homely, lazy odour of bacon fat – the smell of acceptance. There was not much light in the deserted workshop. The host blundered to the wall and switched on a bright naked bulb, up in the ceiling. The three stood blinking at one another for a moment: a coloured man with the fat of the man-of-the-world upon him, grossly dressed – not out of poverty but obviously because he liked it that way – in a rayon sports shirt that gaped and showed two hairy stomach rolls hiding his navel in a lipless grin, the pants of a good suit misbuttoned and held up round the waist by a tie instead of a belt, and a pair of expensive sports shoes, worn without socks; a young Englishman in a worn greenish tweed suit with a neo-Edwardian cut to the waistcoat that labelled it a leftover from undergraduate days; a handsome white woman who, as the light fell upon her, was immediately recognizable to Jake Alexander.

1 **run-down:** heruntergekommen.
4 **tang:** scharfer Geruch, Gestank.
7 **to blunder:** sich ungeschickt bewegen, tappen.
8 **bulb:** Glühbirne.
9 **to blink:** blinzeln.
10 **grossly** (adv.): grob, plump.
12 **rayon:** synthetischer Stoff (wie Nylon).
to gape: offen stehen, klaffen.
13 **navel:** Bauchnabel.
14 **misbuttoned:** falsch zugeknöpft.
17 **tweed:** Tweed (handwebartiger Stoff aus grobem Garn).
18 **to label:** (fig.) kennzeichnen, abstempeln.
19 **undergraduate:** Student.

He had never met her before but he knew the type well – had seen it over and over again at meetings of the Congress of Democrats, and other organizations where progressive whites met progressive blacks. These were the white women who, Jake knew, persisted in regarding themselves as your equal. That was even worse, he thought, than the parsons who persisted in regarding *you* as *their* equal. The parsons had had ten years at school and seven years at a university and theological school; you had carried sacks of vegetables from the market to white people's cars from the time you were eight years old until you were apprenticed to a printer, and your first woman, like your mother, had been a servant, whom you had visited in a backyard room, and your first gulp of whisky, like many of your other pleasures, had been stolen while a white man was not looking. Yet the good parson insisted that your picture of life was exactly the same as his own: *you* felt as *he* did. But these women – oh, Christ! – these women felt as *you* did. They were sure of it. They thought they understood the humiliation of the black man walking the streets only by the permission of a pass written out by a white person, and the guilt and swagger of the coloured man light-faced enough to slink, fugitive from his own skin, into the preserves – the cinemas, bars, libraries – marked "EUROPEANS ONLY". Yes, breathless with stout sensitivity, they insisted on

12 **to be apprenticed to s.o.:** bei jdm. in die Lehre gehen.
14 **gulp:** Schluck.
20 **humiliation:** Demütigung, Erniedrigung.
23 **swagger:** protziges Gehabe, Angeberei.
to slink: schleichen.
24 **fugitive:** flüchtig, auf der Flucht.

walking the whole teeter-totter of the colour line. There was no escaping their understanding. They even insisted on feeling the resentment *you* must feel at their identifying themselves with your feelings ...

Here was the black hair of a determined woman (last year they wore it pulled tightly back into an oddly perched knot; this year it was cropped and curly as a lap dog's), the round, bony brow unpowdered in order to show off the tan, the red mouth, the unrouged cheeks, the big, lively, handsome eyes, dramatically painted, that would look into yours with such intelligent, eager honesty – eager to mirror what Jake Alexander, a big, fat coloured man interested in women, money, brandy and boxing, was feeling. Who the hell wants a woman to look at you honestly, anyway? What has all this to do with a *woman* – with what men and women have for each other in their eyes? She was wearing a wide black skirt, a white cotton blouse baring a good deal of her breasts, and ear-rings that seemed to have been made by a blacksmith out of bits of scrap iron. On her feet she had sandals whose narrow thongs wound between her toes, and the nails of the toes were painted plum colour. By contrast, her hands were neglected-looking – sallow, unmanicured – and on one thin finger there swivelled a

1 **teeter-totter:** Substantiv zu *to teeter* und *to totter* ›schwanken, taumeln, entlangbalancieren‹.
3 **resentment:** Groll, Unwille, Ablehnung.
7 **to perch:** hoch sitzen, kauern.
to crop: stutzen.
19 f. **blacksmith:** Grobschmied.
20 **scrap iron:** Eisenabfall, Schrott.
21 **thong:** Lederriemen.
23 **sallow:** bleich, fahl.
24 **to swivel:** sich herumdrehen.

huge gold seal-ring. She was good-looking, he supposed with disgust.

He stood there, fat, greasy and grinning at the two visitors so lingeringly that his grin looked insolent. Finally he asked, "What brings you this end of town, Mr Halford? Sight-seeing with the lady?"

The young Englishman gave Jake's arm a squeeze, where the short sleeve of the rayon shirt ended. "Just thought I'd look you up, Jake," he said, jolly.

"Come on in, come on in," said Jake on a rising note, shambling ahead of them into the company of the back room. "Here, what about a chair for the lady?" He swept a pile of handbills from the seat of a kitchen chair onto the dusty concrete floor, picked up the chair and planked it down again in the middle of the group of men who had risen awkwardly at the visitors' entrance. "You know Maxie Ndube? And Temba?" Jake said, nodding at two of the men who surrounded him.

Alister Halford murmured with polite warmth his recognition of Maxie, a small, dainty-faced African in neat, businessman's dress, then said inquiringly and hesitantly to Temba, "Have we? When?"

Temba was a coloured man – a mixture of the bloods of black slaves and white masters, blended long ago, in the

4 **insolent:** unverschämt.
7 **to give s.th. a squeeze:** etwas drücken, pressen, quetschen.
11 **to shamble:** schlurfen.
13 **handbill:** Handzettel, Flugblatt.
14 **concrete:** Beton.
14f. **to plank s.th. down:** etwas wie ein Brett hinstellen.
16 **awkwardly** (adv.): ungeschickt, linkisch.
20 **dainty-faced:** mit einem feinen, zierlichen Gesicht.
24 **to blend:** vermischen.

days when the Cape of Good Hope was a port of refreshment for the Dutch East India Company. He was tall and pale, with a large Adam's apple, enormous black eyes, and the look of a musician in a jazz band; you could picture a trumpet lifted to the ceiling in those long yellow hands, that curved spine hunched forward to shield a low note. "In Durban last year, Mr Halford, you remember?" he said eagerly. "I'm sure we met – or perhaps I only saw you there."

"Oh, at the Congress? Of course I remember you!" Halford apologized. "You were in a delegation from the Cape?"

"Miss –?" Jake Alexander waved a hand between the young woman, Maxie, and Temba.

"Jennifer. Jennifer Tetzel," she said again clearly, thrusting out her hand. There was a confused moment when both men reached for it at once and then hesitated, each giving way to the other. Finally the handshaking was accomplished, and the young woman seated herself confidently on the chair.

Jake continued, offhand, "Oh, and of course Billy Boy –" Alister signalled briefly to a black man with sad, blood-shot eyes, who stood awkwardly, back a few steps, against some rolls of paper – "and Klaas and Albert." Klaas and Albert had in their mixed blood some strain of the Bushman, which gave them a batrachian yellowness and toughness, like one of those toads that (prehistoric as

6 **spine:** Rückgrat.
to hunch: krümmen.
21 **offhand:** beiläufig, nebenbei.
23 **blood-shot:** blutunterlaufen.
26 **batrachian:** froschähnlich.
27 **toad:** Kröte.

the Bushman is) are mythically believed to have survived into modern times (hardly more fantastically than the Bushman himself has survived) by spending centuries shut up in an air bubble in a rock. Like Billy Boy, Klaas and Albert had backed away, and, as if abasement against the rolls of paper, the wall or the window were a greeting in itself, the two little coloured men and the big African only stared back at the masculine nods of Alister and the bright smile of the young woman.

"You up from the Cape for anything special now?" Alister said to Temba as he made a place for himself on a corner of a table that was littered with photographic blocks, bits of type, poster proofs, a bottle of souring milk, a bow-tie, a pair of red braces and a number of empty Coca-Cola bottles.

"I've been living in Durban for a year. Just got the chance of a lift to Jo'burg," said the gangling Temba.

Jake had set himself up easily, leaning against the front of the stove and facing Miss Jennifer Tetzel on her chair. He jerked his head towards Temba and said, "Real banana boy." Young white men brought up in the strong Anglo-Saxon tradition of the province of Natal are often referred to, and refer to themselves, as "banana boys", even though fewer and fewer of them have any connection with the dwindling number of vast banana estates that

1 **to survive:** überleben, überdauern.
5 **abasement:** Erniedrigung.
12 **to be littered:** übersät sein.
14 **bow-tie:** Fliege.
braces (pl.): Hosenträger.
17 **gangling:** schlaksig.
20 **to jerk:** ruckartig bewegen.
25 **to dwindle:** schwinden, geringer werden.

once made their owners rich. Jake's broad face, where the bright-pink cheeks of a Highland complexion – inherited, along with his name, from his Scottish father – showed oddly through his coarse, beige skin, creased up in appreciation of his own joke. And Temba threw back his head and laughed, his Adam's apple bobbing, at the idea of himself as a cricket-playing white public-school boy.

"There's nothing like Cape Town, is there?" said the young woman to him, her head charmingly on one side, as if this conviction were something she and he shared.

"Miss Tetzel's up here to look us over. She's from Cape Town," Alister explained.

She turned to Temba with her beauty, her strong provocativeness, full on, as it were. "So we're neighbours?"

Jake rolled one foot comfortably over the other and a spluttering laugh pursed out the pink inner membrane of his lips.

"Where did you live?" she went on, to Temba.

"Cape Flats," he said. Cape Flats is a desolate coloured slum in the bush outside Cape Town.

"Me, too," said the girl, casually.

Temba said politely, "You're kidding." and then looked down uncomfortably at his hands, as if they had been

2 **complexion:** Gesichtsfarbe, Teint.
4 **to crease:** zerknittern, kniffen.
6 **to bob:** sich auf- und abbewegen.
18 **to splutter:** heraussprudeln.
to purse out: herausstülpen.
21 **desolate:** verlassen, einsam, öde.
23 **casually** (adv.): beiläufig, nebenbei.
24 **you're kidding:** das ist nicht dein Ernst!

guilty of some clumsy movement. He had not meant to sound so familiar; the words were not the right ones.

"I've been there nearly ten months," she said.

"Well, some people've got queer tastes," Jake remarked, laughing, to no one in particular, as if she were not there.

"How's that?" Temba was asking her shyly, respectfully.

She mentioned the name of a social rehabilitation scheme that was in operation in the slum. "I'm assistant director of the thing at the moment. It's connected with the sort of work I do at the university, you see, so they've given me fifteen months' leave from my usual job."

Maxie noticed with amusement the way she used the word "job", as if she were a plumber's mate; he and his educated African friends – journalists and schoolteachers – were careful to talk only of their "professions". "Good works," he said, smiling quietly.

She planted her feet comfortably before her, wriggling on the hard chair, and said to Temba with mannish frankness, "It's a ghastly place. How in God's name did you survive living there? I don't think I can last out more than another few months, and I've always got my flat in Cape Town to escape to on Sundays, and so on."

While Temba smiled, turning his protruding eyes aside slowly, Jake looked straight at her and said, "Then why do you, lady, why *do* you?"

1 **clumsy:** unbeholfen, plump.
15 **plumber:** Klempner, Installateur.
19 **to wriggle:** sich winden, hin- und herdrehen.
20 **mannish:** männlich, maskulin.
21 **ghastly:** gräßlich, grausig.
25 **to protrude:** vorstehen, herausragen.

"Oh, I don't know. Because I don't see why anyone else – any one of the people who live there – should have to, I suppose." She laughed before anyone else could at the feebleness, the philanthropic uselessness of what she was saying. "Guilt, what-have-you . . ."

Maxie shrugged, as if at the mention of some expensive illness he had never been able to afford and whose symptoms he could not imagine.

There was a moment of silence; the two coloured men and the big black man standing back against the wall watched anxiously, as if some sort of signal might be expected, possibly from Jake Alexander, their boss, the man who, like themselves, was not white, yet who owned his own business and had a car and money and strange friends – sometimes even white people, such as these. The three of them were dressed in the ill-matched cast-off clothing that all humble workpeople who are not white wear in Johannesburg, and they had not lost the ability of rural people to stare, unembarrassed and unembarrassing.

Jake winked at Alister; it was one of his mannerisms – a bookie's wink, a stage comedian's wink. "Well, how's it going, boy, how's it going?" he said. His turn of phrase was bar-room bonhomie; with luck, he *could* get into a bar, too. With a hat to cover his hair and his coat collar well up, and only a bit of greasy pink cheek showing, he

4 **philanthropic:** philanthropisch, menschenfreundlich.
6 **to shrug:** die Achseln zucken.
19 **rural:** ländlich.
to unembarrass: nicht verwirren, nicht in Verlegenheit bringen.
21 **mannerism:** Eigenheit, Manieriertheit.
22 **bookie:** Buchmacher.
24 **bonhomie:** überströmende Freundlichkeit.

had slipped into the bars of the shabbier Johannesburg hotels with Alister many times and got away with it. Alister, on the other hand, had got away with the same sort of thing narrowly several times, too, when he had accompanied Jake to a shebeen in a coloured location, where it was illegal for a white man to be, as well as illegal for anyone at all to have a drink; twice Alister had escaped a raid by jumping out of a window. Alister had been in South Africa only eighteen months, as correspondent for a newspaper in England, and because he was only two or three years away from undergraduate escapades such incidents seemed to give him a kind of nostalgic pleasure; he found them funny. Jake, for his part, had decided long ago (with the great help of the money he had made) that he would take the whole business of the colour bar as humorous. The combination of these two attitudes, stemming from such immeasurably different circumstances, had the effect of making their friendship less self-conscious than is usual between a white man and a coloured one.

"They tell me it's going to be a good thing on Saturday night?" said Alister, in the tone of questioning someone in the know. He was referring to a boxing match between two coloured heavyweights, one of whom was a protégé of Jake.

Jake grinned deprecatingly, like a fond mother. "Well,

1 **shabby:** schäbig.
5 **shebeen:** illegale Verkaufsstelle für Alkohol.
location: Siedlung für Schwarze, meist in der Nähe einer Kleinstadt.
8 **raid:** Überfall, Razzia.
17 **immeasurably** (adv.): unermeßlich.
24 **protégé:** Schützling.
26 **to deprecate:** mißbilligen, verurteilen.

Pikkie's a good boy," he said. "I tell you, it'll be something to see." He danced about a little on his clumsy toes in pantomime of the way a boxer nimbles himself, and collapsed against the stove, his belly shaking with laughter at his breathlessness.

"Too much smoking, too many brandies, Jake," said Alister.

"With me, it's too many women, boy."

"We were just congratulating Jake," said Maxie in his soft, precise voice, the indulgent, tongue-in-cheek tone of the protégé who is superior to his patron, for Maxie was one of Jake's boys, too – of a different kind. Though Jake had decided that for him being on the wrong side of a colour bar was ludicrous, he was as indulgent to those who took it seriously and politically, the way Maxie did, as he was to any up-and-coming youngster who, say, showed talent in the ring or wanted to go to America and become a singer. They could all make themselves free of Jake's pocket, and his printing shop, and his room in the lower end of the town, where the building had fallen below the standard of white people but was far superior to the kind of thing most coloureds and blacks were accustomed to.

"Congratulations on what?" the young white woman asked. She had a way of looking up around her, questioningly, from face to face, that came of long familiarity with being the centre of attention at parties.

3 **to nimble o.s.:** sich gelenkig machen.
4 **belly:** Bauch.
10 **tongue-in-cheek:** verschmitzt, spöttisch.
14 **ludicrous:** lächerlich.
16 **up-and-coming:** aufstrebend, heranwachsend.
youngster: Junge, Jüngling.

"Yes, you can shake my hand, boy," said Jake to Alister. "I didn't see it, but these fellows tell me that my divorce went through. It's in the papers today."

"Is that so? But from what I hear, you won't be a free man long," Alister said teasingly.

Jake giggled, and pressed at one gold-filled tooth with a strong fingernail. "You heard about the little parcel I'm expecting from Zululand?" he asked.

"Zululand?" said Alister. "I thought your Lila came from Stellenbosch."

Maxie and Temba laughed.

"Lila? *What* Lila?" said Jake with exaggerated innocence.

"You're behind the times," said Maxie to Alister.

"You know I like them – well, sort of round," said Jake. "Don't care for the thin kind, in the long run."

"But Lila had red hair!" Alister goaded him. He remembered the incongruously dyed, straightened hair on a fine coloured girl whose nostrils dilated in the manner of certain fleshy water-plants seeking prey.

Jennifer Tetzel got up and turned the gas off on the stove, behind Jake. "That bacon'll be like charred string," she said.

Jake did not move – merely looked at her lazily. "This is

2 **divorce:** Ehescheidung.
5 **to tease:** necken, hänseln.
12 **to exaggerate:** übertreiben.
17 **to goad s.o.:** jdn. aufreizen, anstacheln.
18 **incongruously** (adv.): nicht zusammenpassend.
to dye: färben.
19 **nostril:** Nasenloch.
to dilate: sich ausdehnen.
22 **charred:** verkohlt.

not the way to talk with a lady around." He grinned, unapologetic.

She smiled at him and sat down, shaking her ear-rings. "Oh, I'm divorced myself. Are we keeping you people from your supper? Do go ahead and eat. Don't bother about us."

Jake turned around, gave the shrunken rashers a mild shake and put the pan aside. "Hell, no," he said. "Any time. But –" turning to Alister – "won't you have something to eat?" He looked about, helpless and unconcerned, as if to indicate an absence of plates and a general careless lack of equipment such as white women would be accustomed to use when they ate. Alister said quickly, no, he had promised to take Jennifer to Moorjee's.

Of course, Jake should have known; a woman like that would *want* to be taken to eat at an Indian place in Vrededorp, even though she was white, and free to eat at the best hotel in town. He felt suddenly, after all, the old gulf opening between himself and Alister: what did *they* see in such women – bristling, sharp, all-seeing, knowing women, who talked like men, who wanted to show all the time that, apart from sex, they were exactly the same as men? He looked at Jennifer and her clothes, and thought of the way a white woman could look: one of those big, soft, European women with curly yellow hair, with very high-heeled shoes that made them shake softly when they walked, with a strong scent, like hot flowers, coming

2 **unapologetic:** nicht zur Entschuldigung bereit, störrisch.
5 **to bother:** sich kümmern.
7 **rasher:** Speckstreifen.
20 **to bristle:** sich sträuben.
27 **scent:** Geruch, Duft.

up, it seemed, from their jutting breasts under the lace and pink and blue and all the other pretty things they wore – women with nothing resistant about them except, buried in white, boneless fingers, those red, pointed nails that scratched faintly at your palms.

"You should have been along with me at lunch today," said Maxie to no one in particular. Or perhaps the soft voice, a vocal tiptoe, was aimed at Alister, who was familiar with Maxie's work as an organizer of African trade unions. The group in the room gave him their attention (Temba with the little encouraging grunt of one who has already heard the story), but Maxie paused a moment, smiling ruefully at what he was about to tell. Then he said, "You know George Elson?" Alister nodded. The man was a white lawyer who had been arrested twice for his participation in anti-colour-bar movements.

"Oh, George? I've worked with George often in Cape Town," put in Jennifer.

"Well," continued Maxie, "George Elson and I went out to one of the industrial towns on the East Rand. We were interviewing the bosses, you see, not the men, and at the beginning it was all right, though, once or twice the girls in the offices thought I was George's driver – 'Your boy can wait outside." He laughed, showing small, perfect

1 **to jut:** hervorstehen, herausragen.
5 **palm:** Handinnenfläche.
8 **vocal:** stimmlich.
tiptoe: Substantiv zu *to tiptoe* ›auf Zehenspitzen gehen‹.
10 **trade unions:** Gewerkschaften.
11 **grunt:** Grunzen, Murren.
13 **ruefully** (adv.): reuig, kläglich, traurig.
16 **participation:** Teilnahme.

teeth; everything about him was finely made – his straight-fingered dark hands, the curved African nostrils of his small nose, his little ears, which grew close to the sides of his delicate head. The others were silent, but the young woman laughed, too.

"We even got tea in one place," Maxie went on. "One of the girls came in with two cups and a tin mug. But old George took the mug."

Jennifer Tetzel laughed again, knowingly.

"Then, just about lunch time, we came to this place I wanted to tell you about. Nice chap, the manager. Never blinked an eye at me, called me Mister. And after we'd talked, he said to George, 'Why not come home with me for lunch?' So of course George said, 'Thanks, but I'm with my friend here.' 'Oh, that's O.K.,' said the chap. 'Bring him along.' Well, we go along to this house, and the chap disappears into the kitchen, and then he comes back and we sit in the lounge and have a beer, and then the servant comes along and says lunch is ready. Just as we're walking into the dining room, the chap takes me by the arm and says, 'I've had *your* lunch laid on a table on the stoep. You'll find it's all perfectly clean and nice, just what we're having ourselves.'"

"Fantastic," murmured Alister.

Maxie smiled and shrugged, looking around at them all. "It's true."

"After he'd asked you, and he'd sat having a drink with you?" Jennifer said closely, biting in her lower lip, as if this were a problem to be solved psychologically.

7 **mug:** Krug, Kanne, Becher.
11 **chap:** Bursche, Kerl.
22 **stoep** (S.Afr.): Veranda.

"Of course," said Maxie.

Jake was shaking with laughter, like some obscene Silenus. There was no sound out of him, but saliva gleamed on his lips, and his belly, at the level of Jennifer Tetzel's eyes, was convulsed.

Temba said soberly, in the tone of one whose goodwill makes it difficult for him to believe in the unease of his situation, "I certainly find it worse here than at the Cape. I can't remember, y'know, about buses. I keep getting put off European buses."

Maxie pointed to Jake's heaving belly. "Oh, I'll tell you a better one than that," he said. "Something that happened in the office one day. Now, the trouble with me is, apparently, I don't talk like a native." This time everyone laughed, except Maxie himself, who, with the instinct of a good raconteur, kept a polite, modest, straight face.

"You know that's true," interrupted the young white woman. "You have none of the usual softening of the vowels of most Africans. And you haven't got an Afrikaans accent, as some Africans have, even if they get rid of the African thing."

"Anyway, I'd had to phone a certain firm several times," Maxie went on, "and I'd got to know the voice of the girl

2 **obscene:** obszön, unanständig.
3 **Silenus:** Silen (in der griechischen Mythologie pferdegestaltiger Dämon, von dem wesensähnlichen Sartyr nicht unterscheidbar).
saliva: Speichel, Spucke.
5 **to convulse:** in Zuckungen versetzen, erschüttern.
7 **unease:** Unbehaglichkeit.
11 **to heave:** sich heben und senken.
16 **raconteur:** Geschichtenerzähler, Plauderer.
20 **vowel:** Vokal.

at the other end, and she'd got to know mine. As a matter of fact, she must have liked the sound of me, because she was getting very friendly. We fooled about a bit, exchanged first names, like a couple of kids – hers was Peggy – and she said, eventually, 'Aren't you ever going to come to the office yourself?'" Maxie paused a moment, and his tongue flicked at the side of his mouth in a brief, nervous gesture. When he spoke again, his voice was flat, like the voice of a man who is telling a joke and suddenly thinks that perhaps it is not such a good one after all. "So I told her I'd be in next day, about four. I walked in, sure enough, just as I said I would. She was a pretty girl, blonde, you know, with very tidy hair – I guessed she'd just combed it to be ready for me. She looked up and said 'Yes?' holding out her hand for the messenger's book or parcel she thought I'd brought. I took her hand and shook it and said, 'Well, here I am, on time – I'm Maxie – Maxie Ndube.'"

"What'd she do?" asked Temba eagerly.

The interruption seemed to restore Maxie's confidence in his story. He shrugged gaily. "She almost dropped my hand, and then she pumped it like a mad thing, and her neck and ears went so red I thought she'd burn up. Honestly, her ears were absolutely shining. She tried to pretend she'd known all along, but I could see she was terrified someone would come from the inner office and see her shaking hands with a native. So I took pity on her and went away. Didn't even stay for my appointment with

5 **eventually** (adv.): schließlich, endlich.
7 **to flick:** züngeln, schnalzen.
20 **to restore:** wiederherstellen.
25 f. **to be terrified:** sich fürchten.

her boss. When I went back to keep the postponed appointment the next week, we pretended we'd never met."

Temba was slapping his knee. "God, I'd have loved to see her face!" he said.

Jake wiped away a tear from his fat cheek – his eyes were light blue, and produced tears easily when he laughed – and said, "That'll teach you not to talk swanky, man. Why can't you talk like the rest of us?"

"Oh, I'll watch out on the 'Missus' and 'Baas' stuff in future," said Maxie.

Jennifer Tetzel cut into their laughter with her cool, practical voice. "Poor little girl, she probably liked you awfully, Maxie, and was really disappointed. You mustn't be too harsh on her. It's hard to be punished for not being black."

The moment was one of astonishment rather than irritation. Even Jake, who had been sure that there could be no possible situation between white and black he could not find amusing, only looked quickly from the young woman to Maxie, in a hiatus between anger, which he had given up long ago, and laughter, which suddenly failed him. On his face was admiration more than anything else – sheer, grudging admiration. This one was the best yet. This one was the coolest ever.

"Is it?" said Maxie to Jennifer, pulling in the corners of his mouth and regarding her from under slightly raised

1 **to postpone:** aufschieben, verschieben.
4 **to slap:** klopfen, einen Klaps geben.
8 **to talk swanky:** großspurig daherreden.
10 **baas** (Afrik.): Herr, Boss.
21 **hiatus:** Lücke, Unterbrechung.
24 **grudging:** widerwillig (*to grudge:* mißgönnen).

eyebrows. Jake watched. Oh, she'd have a hard time with Maxie. Maxie wouldn't give up his suffering-tempered blackness so easily. You hadn't much hope of knowing what Maxie was feeling at any given moment, because Maxie not only never let you know but made you guess wrong. But this one was the best yet.

She looked back at Maxie, opening her eyes very wide, twisting her sandalled foot on the swivel of its ankle, smiling. "Really, I assure you it is."

Maxie bowed to her politely, giving way with a falling gesture of his hand.

Alister had slid from his perch on the crowded table, and now, prodding Jake playfully in the paunch, he said, "We have to get along."

Jake scratched his ear and said again, "Sure you won't have something to eat?"

Alister shook his head. "We had hoped you'd offer us a drink, but –"

Jake wheezed with laughter, but this time was sincerely concerned. "Well, to tell you the truth, when we heard the knocking, we just swallowed the last of the bottle off, in case it was someone it shouldn't be. I haven't a drop in the place till tomorrow. Sorry, chappie. Must apologize to you, lady, but we black men've got to drink in secret. If we'd've known it was you two . . ."

Maxie and Temba hat risen. The two wizened coloured

8 **swivel:** Drehpunkt.
12 **perch:** Sitzplatz.
13 **to prod s.o.:** jdn. anstoßen, jdm. einen Schubs geben.
paunch: Bauch, Wanst.
19 **to wheeze:** pfeifend atmen, keuchen.
23 **chappie:** Kumpel, Kerl.
26 **wizened:** verschrumpelt, verhutzelt.

men, Klaas and Albert, and the sombre black Billy Boy shuffled helplessly, hanging about.
Alister said, "Next time, Jake, next time. We'll give you fair warning and you can lay it on."
Jennifer shook hands with Temba and Maxie, called "Good-bye! Good-bye!" to the others, as if they were somehow out of earshot in that small room. From the door, she suddenly said to Maxie, "I feel I must tell you. About that other story – your first one, about the lunch. I don't believe it. I'm sorry, but I honestly don't. It's too illogical to hold water."
It was the final self-immolation by honest understanding. There was absolutely no limit to which that understanding would not go. Even if she could not believe Maxie, she must keep her determined good faith with him by confessing her disbelief. She would go to the length of calling him a liar to show by frankness how much she respected him – to insinuate, perhaps, that she was *with him*, even in the need to invent something about a white man that she, because she herself was white, could not believe. It was her last bid for Maxie.
The small, perfectly-made man crossed his arms and smiled, watching her go. Maxie had no price.
Jake saw his guests out of the shop, and switched off the light after he had closed the door behind them. As he walked back through the dark, where his presses smelled

1 **sombre:** dunkel, düster.
2 **to shuffle:** schlurfen.
4 **to lay it on:** etwas ‚auffahren'.
7 **out of earshot:** außer Hörweite.
11 **to hold water** (fig.): stimmig, überzeugend sein.
12 **self-immolation:** Selbstopfer.
18 **to insinuate:** andeuten, zu erkennen geben.

metallic and cool, he heard, for a few moments, the clear voice of the white woman and the low, noncommittal English murmur of Alister, his friend, as they went out through the archway into the street.

He blinked a little as he came back to the light and the faces that confronted him in the back room. Klaas had taken the dirty glasses from behind the curtain and was holding them one by one under the tap in the sink. Billy Boy and Albert had come closer out of the shadows and were leaning their elbows on a roll of paper. Temba was sitting on the table, swinging his foot. Maxie had not moved, and stood just as he had, with his arms folded. No one spoke.

Jake began to whistle softly through the spaces between his front teeth, and he picked up the pan of bacon, looked at the twisted curls of meat, jellied now in cold white fat, and put it down again absently. He stood a moment, heavily, regarding them all, but no one responded. His eye encountered the chair that he had cleared for Jennifer Tetzel to sit on. Suddenly he kicked it, hard, so that it went flying on to its side. Then, rubbing his big hands together and bursting into loud whistling to accompany an impromptu series of dance steps, he said "Now, boys!" and as they stirred, he planked the pan down on the ring and turned the gas up till it roared beneath it.

2 **noncommittal:** zurückhaltend, vorsichtig.
16 **twisted:** verknäult.
jellied: zu Gelee geworden.
17 **absently** (adv.): geistesabwesend.
19 **to encounter:** begegnen, treffen.
23 **impromptu:** improvisiert.

Town and Country Lovers

One

Dr Franz-Josef von Leinsdorf is a geologist absorbed in his work; wrapped up in it, as the saying goes – year after year the experience of this work enfolds him, swaddling him away from the landscapes, the cities and the people, wherever he lives: Peru, New Zealand, the United States. He's always been like that, his mother could confirm from their native Austria. There, even as a handsome small boy he presented only his profile to her: turned away to his bits of rock and stone. His few relaxations have not changed much since then. An occasional skiing trip, listening to music, reading poetry – Rainer Maria Rilke once stayed in his grandmother's hunting lodge in the forests of Styria and the boy was introduced to Rilke's poems while very young.

Layer upon layer, country after country, wherever his work takes him – and now he has been almost seven years in Africa. First the Côte d'Ivoire, and for the past five years, South Africa. The shortage of skilled manpower

5 **to enfold:** umschlingen, umfassen.
to swaddle: umwickeln, einpacken.
11 f. **relaxation:** Entspannung, Erholung.
14 f. **hunting lodge:** Jagdhütte.
15 **Styria:** Steiermark (österreichisches Bundesland).
17 **layer:** Schicht, Lage.
19 **Côte d'Ivoire** (Fr.): Elfenbeinküste.
20 **skilled manpower:** gelernte Arbeitskräfte, Facharbeiter.

brought about his recruitment here. He has no interest in the politics of the countries he works in. His private preoccupation-within-the-preoccupation of his work has been research into underground water-courses, but the mining company that employs him in a senior though not executive capacity is interested only in mineral discovery. So he is much out in the field – which is the veld, here – seeking new gold, copper, platinum and uranium deposits. When he is at home – on this particular job, in this particular country, this city – he lives in a two-roomed flat in a suburban block with a landscaped garden, and does his shopping at a supermarket conveniently across the street. He is not married – yet. That is how his colleagues, and the typists and secretaries at the mining company's head office, would define his situation. Both men and women would describe him as a good-looking man, in a foreign way, with the lower half of the face dark and middle-aged (his mouth is thin and curving, and no matter how close-shaven his beard shows like fine shot embedded in the skin round mouth and chin) and the upper half contradictorily young, with deep-set eyes (some would say grey, some black), thick eyelashes and brows. A tangled gaze: through which concentration and gleaming thoughtfulness perhaps appear as fire and languor. It is this that the women in the office

1 **recruitment:** Ein-, Anstellung.
4 **research:** Forschung.
6 **executive capacity:** Führungsposition.
7 **veld:** offenes Grasland in Südafrika.
9 **deposits:** Ablagerungen.
20 **shot:** Schrot.
21 **contradictorily** (adv.): entgegengesetzt, im Widerspruch stehend.
23 **to tangle:** verwirren.
25 **languor:** Mattigkeit, Dumpfheit, Schlaffheit.

mean when they remark he's not unattractive. Although the gaze seems to promise, he has never invited any one of them to go out with him. There is the general assumption he probably has a girl who's been picked for him, he's bespoken by one of his own kind, back home in Europe where he comes from. Many of these well-educated Europeans have no intention of becoming permanent immigrants; neither the remnant of white colonial life nor idealistic involvement with Black Africa appeals to them.

One advantage, at least, of living in underdeveloped or half-developed countries is that flats are serviced. All Dr von Leinsdorf has to do for himself is buy his own supplies and cook an evening meal if he doesn't want to go to a restaurant. It is simply a matter of dropping in to the supermarket on his way from his car to his flat after work in the afternoon. He wheels a trolley up and down the shelves, and his simple needs are presented to him in the form of tins, packages, plastic-wrapped meat, cheeses, fruit and vegetables, tubes, bottles ... At the cashiers' counters where customers must converge and queue there are racks of small items uncategorized, for last-minute purchase. Here, as the coloured girl cashier punches the adding machine, he picks up cigarettes and perhaps a packet of salted nuts or a bar of nougat. Or

4 **to pick:** aussuchen.
5 **to bespeak:** im voraus bitten.
8 **remnant:** Überrest, Überbleibsel.
17 **trolley:** Einkaufswagen.
21 **to converge:** zusammenlaufen, sich annähern.
to queue: Schlange stehen.
22 **uncategorized:** nicht eingeordnet.
24 **to punch:** drücken.

razor-blades, when he remembers he's running short. One evening in winter he saw that the cardboard display was empty of the brand of blades he preferred, and he drew the cashier's attention to this. These young coloured girls are usually pretty unhelpful, taking money and punching their machines in a manner that asserts with the time-serving obstinacy of the half-literate the limit of any responsibility towards customers, but this one ran an alert glance over the selection of razor-blades, apologized that she was not allowed to leave her post, and said she would see that the stock was replenished "next time". A day or two later she recognized him, gravely, as he took his turn before her counter – "I ahssed them, but it's out of stock. You can't get it. I did ahss about it." He said this didn't matter. "When it comes in, I can keep a few packets for you." He thanked her.

He was away with the prospectors the whole of the next week. He arrived back in town just before nightfall on Friday, and was on his way from car to flat with his arms full of briefcase, suitcase and canvas bags when someone stopped him by standing timidly in his path. He was about to dodge round unseeingly on the crowded pavement but she spoke. "We got the blades in now. I didn't see you in the shop this week, but I kept some for when you come. So . . ."

He recognized her. He had never seen her standing

7 **obstinacy:** Halsstarrigkeit, Bockigkeit.
9 **alert:** wachsam, munter.
11 **to replenish:** auffüllen.
13 **ahssed:** *asked.*
17 **prospector:** Gold-, Erz-, Ölsucher.
20 **canvas:** Segel-, Zelttuch.
22 **to dodge:** ausweichen.

before, and she was wearing a coat. She was rather small and finely-made, for one of them. The coat was skimpy but no big backside jutted. The cold brought an apricot-graining of warm colour to her cheek-bones, beneath which a very small face was quite delicately hollowed, and the skin was smooth, the subdued satiny colour of certain yellow wood. That crêpey hair, but worn drawn back flat and in a little knot pushed into one of the cheap wool chignons that (he recognized also) hung in the miscellany of small goods along with the razor-blades, at the supermarket. He said thanks, he was in a hurry, he'd only just got back from a trip – shifting the burdens he carried, to demonstrate. "Oh shame." She acknowledged his load. "But if you want I can run in and get it for you quickly. If you want."

He saw at once it was perfectly clear that all the girl meant was that she would go back to the supermarket, buy the blades and bring the packet to him there where he stood, on the pavement. And it seemed that it was this certainty that made him say, in the kindly tone of assumption used for an obliging underling, "I live just across there – *Atlantis* – that flat building. Could you drop them by, for me – number seven-hundred-and-eighteen, seventh floor –"

She had not before been inside one of these big flat build-

2 **skimpy:** dürftig, kläglich.
3 **to jut:** hervorstehen, herausragen.
6 **subdued:** gedämpft, bedrückt.
satiny: aus (Atlas-)Seide, seidig.
7 **crêpey:** (wie Krepp) gewellt.
9 **chignon:** Haarknoten, Zopf.
9 f. **miscellany:** Gemisch, Potpourri.
21 **assumption:** Anmaßung.

ings near where she worked. She lived a bus- and train-ride away to the West of the city, but this side of the black townships, in a township for people her tint. There was a pool with ferns, not plastic, and even a little waterfall pumped electrically over rocks, in the entrance of the building *Atlantis*; she didn't wait for the lift marked GOODS but took the one meant for whites and a white woman with one of those sausage-dogs on a lead got in with her but did not pay her any attention. The corridors leading to the flats were nicely glassed-in, not draughty.

He wondered if he should give her a twenty-cent piece for her trouble – ten cents would be right for a black; but she said, "Oh no – please, here –" standing outside his open door and awkwardly pushing back at his hand the change from the money he'd given her for the razor-blades. She was smiling, for the first time, in the dignity of refusing a tip. It was difficult to know how to treat these people, in this country; to know what they expected. In spite of her embarrassing refusal of the coin, she stood there, completely unassuming, fists thrust down the pockets of her cheap coat against the cold she'd come in from, rather pretty thin legs neatly aligned, knee to knee, ankle to ankle.

"Would you like a cup of coffee or something?"

3 **township:** von der Südafrikanischen Regierung angelegte Siedlung für Schwarze.
tint: Farbe.
4 **fern:** Farnkraut.
15 **awkwardly** (adv.): linkisch, verlegen.
18 **tip:** Trinkgeld.
20 **to embarrass:** in Verlegenheit bringen.
23 **to align:** ausrichten, in eine Linie bringen.

He couldn't very well take her into his study-cum-living-room and offer her a drink. She followed him to his kitchen, but at the sight of her pulling out the single chair to drink her cup of coffee at the kitchen table, he said, "No – bring it in here –" and led the way into the big room where, among his books and his papers, his files of scientific correspondence (and the cigar boxes of stamps from the envelopes) his racks of records, his specimens of minerals and rocks, he lived alone.

It was no trouble to her; she saved him the trips to the supermarket and brought him his groceries two or three times a week. All he had to do was to leave a list and the key under the doormat, and she would come up in her lunch-hour to collect them, returning to put his supplies in the flat after work. Sometimes he was home and sometimes not. He bought a box of chocolates and left it, with a note, for her to find; and that was acceptable, apparently, as a gratuity.

Her eyes went over everything in the flat although her body tried to conceal its sense of being out of place by remaining as still as possible, holding its contours in the chair offered her as a stranger's coat is set aside and remains exactly as left until the owner takes it up to go.

"You collect?"

"Well, these are specimens – connected with my work."

"My brother used to collect. Miniatures. With brandy and whisky and that, in them. From all over. Different countries."

8 **specimen:** Muster, Probestück, Exemplar.
18 **gratuity:** Sonderzuwendung, Trinkgeld.
26 **miniatures:** Reklamebilder.

The second time she watched him grinding coffee for the cup he had offered her she said, "You always do that? Always when you make coffee?"

"But of course. Is it no good, for you? Do I make it too strong?"

"Oh it's just I'm not used to it. We buy it ready – you know, it's in a bottle, you just add a bit to the milk or water."

He laughed, instructive: "That's not coffee, that's a synthetic flavouring. In my country we drink only real coffee, fresh, from the beans – you smell how good it is as it's being ground?"

She was stopped by the caretaker and asked what she wanted in the building? Heavy with the *bona fides* of groceries clutched to her body, she said she was working at number 718, on the seventh floor. The caretaker did not tell her not to use the whites' lift; after all, she was not black; her family was very light-skinned.

There was the item "grey button for trousers" on one of his shopping lists. She said as she unpacked the supermarket carrier, "Give me the pants, so long, then," and sat on his sofa that was always gritty with fragments of pipe tobacco, sewing in and out through the four holes of the button with firm, fluent movements of the right hand, gestures supplying the articulacy missing from her talk.

10 **to flavour:** Geruch oder Geschmack geben.
13 **caretaker:** Hausmeister, Verwalter.
14 **bona fides** (lat.): Rechtmäßigkeit.
15 **to clutch:** drücken, greifen, packen.
21 **carrier:** Tragetasche.
pants (pl.): Hose.
22 **gritty:** krümelig, bekrümelt.
25 **articulacy:** Artikuliertheit, Ausdrucksfähigkeit.

She had a little yokel's, peasant's (he thought of it) gap between her two front teeth when she smiled that he didn't much like, but, face ellipsed to three-quarter angle, eyes cast down in concentration with soft lips almost closed, this didn't matter. He said, watching her sew, "You're a good girl"; and touched her.

She remade the bed every late afternoon when they left it and she dressed again before she went home. After a week there was a day when late afternoon became evening, and they were still in the bed.

"Can't you stay the night?"

"My mother," she said.

"Phone her. Make an excuse." He was a foreigner. He had been in the country five years, but he didn't understand that people don't usually have telephones in their houses, where she lived. She got up to dress. He didn't want that tender body to go out in the night cold and kept hindering her with the interruption of his hands; saying nothing. Before she put on her coat, when the body had already disappeared, he spoke. "But you must make some arrangement."

"Oh my mother!" Her face opened to fear and vacancy he could not read.

He was not entirely convinced the woman would think of her daughter as some pure and unsullied virgin ... "Why?"

The girl said, "S'e'll be scared. S'e'll be scared we get caught."

1 **yokel:** Bauerntölpel.
22 **vacancy:** Leere.
25 **unsullied:** unbefleckt, nicht beschmutzt.

"Don't tell her anything. Say I'm employing you." In this country he was working in now there were generally rooms on the roofs of flat buildings for tenants' servants.

She said: "That's what I told the caretaker."

She ground fresh coffee beans every time he wanted a cup while he was working at night. She never attempted to cook anything until she had watched in silence while he did it the way he liked, and she learned to reproduce exactly the simple dishes he preferred. She handled his pieces of rock and stone, at first admiring the colours – "It'd make a beautiful ring or a necklace, ay." Then he showed her the striations, the formation of each piece, and explained what each was, and how, in the long life of the earth, it had been formed. He named the mineral it yielded, and what that was used for. He worked at his papers, writing, writing, every night, so it did not matter that they could not go out together to public places. On Sundays she got into his car in the basement garage and they drove to the country and picnicked away up in the Magaliesberg, where there was no one. He read or poked about among the rocks; they climbed together, to the mountain pools. He taught her to swim. She had never seen the sea. She squealed and shrieked in the water, showing the gap between her teeth, as – it crossed his mind – she must do when among her own people. Occasionally he had to go out to dinner at the houses of collea-

3 **tenant:** Mieter.
13 **striation:** Streifenmuster.
21 f. **to poke about:** herumstochern.
24 **to squeal:** kreischen, quietschen.

gues from the mining company; she sewed and listened to the radio in the flat and he found her in the bed, warm and already asleep, by the time he came in. He made his way into her body without speaking; she made him welcome without a word. Once he put on evening dress for a dinner at his country's consulate; watching him brush one or two fallen hairs from the shoulders of the dark jacket that sat so well on him, she saw a huge room, all chandeliers and people dancing some dance from a costume film – stately, hand-to-hand. She supposed he was going to fetch, in her place in the car, a partner for the evening. They never kissed when either left the flat; he said, suddenly, kindly, pausing as he picked up cigarettes and keys, "Don't be lonely." And added, "Wouldn't you like to visit your family sometimes, when I have to go out?"

He had told her he was going home to his mother in the forests and mountains of his country near the Italian border (he showed her on the map) after Christmas. She had not told him how her mother, not knowing there was any other variety, assumed he was a medical doctor, so she had talked to her about the doctor's children and the doctor's wife who was a very kind lady, glad to have someone who could help out in the surgery as well as the flat.

She remarked wonderingly on his ability to work until midnight or later, after a day at work. She was so tired when she came home from her cash register at the supermarket that once dinner was eaten she could scarcely keep awake. He explained in a way she could understand

9 **chandelier:** Kronleuchter.
24 **surgery:** Arztpraxis.

that while the work she did was repetitive, undemanding of any real response from her intelligence, requiring little mental or physical effort and therefore unrewarding, his work was his greatest interest, it taxed his mental capacities to their limit, exercised all his concentration, and rewarded him constantly as much with the excitement of a problem presented as with the satisfaction of a problem solved. He said later, putting away his papers, speaking out of a silence: "Have you done other kinds of work?" She said, "I was in a clothing factory before. Sportbeau shirts; you know? But the pay's better in the shop."

Of course. Being a conscientious newspaper-reader in every country he lived in, he was aware that it was only recently that the retail consumer trade in this one had been allowed to employ coloureds as shop assistants; even punching a cash register represented advancement. With the continuing shortage of semi-skilled whites a girl like this might be able to edge a little farther into the white-collar category. He began to teach her to type. He was aware that her English was poor, even though, as a foreigner, in his ears her pronunciation did not offend, nor categorize her as it would in those of someone of his education whose mother tongue was English. He corrected her grammatical mistakes but missed the less obvious ones because of his own sometimes exotic English usage – she continued to use the singular pronoun "it" when what was required was the plural "they". Because

4 **to tax:** prüfen, beanspruchen.
13 **conscientious:** gewissenhaft.
15 **retail consumer trade:** Einzelhandel.
18 **shortage:** Knappheit, Mangel.

he was a foreigner (although so clever, as she saw) she was less inhibited than she might have been by the words she knew she misspelled in her typing. While she sat at the typewriter she thought how one day she would type notes for him, as well as making coffee the way he liked it, and taking him inside her body without saying anything, and sitting (even if only through the empty streets of quiet Sundays) beside him in his car, like a wife.

On a summer night near Christmas – he had already bought and hidden a slightly showy but nevertheless good watch he thought she would like – there was a knocking at the door that brought her out of the bathroom and him to his feet, at his work-table. No one ever came to the flat at night; he had no friends intimate enough to drop in without warning. The summons was an imperious banging that did not pause and clearly would not stop until the door was opened.

She stood in the open bathroom doorway gazing at him across the passage into the living-room; her bare feet and shoulders were free of a big bath-towel. She said nothing, did not even whisper. The flat seemed to shake with the strong unhurried blows.

He made as if to go to the door, at last, but now she ran and clutched him by both arms. She shook her head wildly; her lips drew back but her teeth were clenched, she didn't speak. She pulled him into the bedroom, snatched some clothes from the clean laundry laid out on

2 **inhibited:** gehemmt.
10 **showy:** protzig, angeberisch.
16 **imperious:** gebieterisch, herrisch, dringend.
25 **to clench:** zusammenpressen.
27 **laundry:** Wäsche.

the bed and got into the wall-cupboard, thrusting the key at his hand. Although his arms and calves felt weakly cold he was horrified, distastefully embarrassed at the sight of her pressed back crouching there under his suits and coat; it was horrible and ridiculous. *Come out!* he whispered. *No! Come out!* She hissed: *Where? Where can I go?*

Never mind! Get out of there!

He put out his hand to grasp her. At bay, she said with all the force of her terrible whisper, baring the gap in her teeth: *I'll throw myself out the window.*

She forced the key into his hand like the handle of a knife. He closed the door on her face and drove the key home in the lock, then dropped it among coins in his trouser pocket.

He unslotted the chain that was looped across the flat door. He turned the serrated knob of the Yale lock. The three policemen, two in plain clothes, stood there without impatience although they had been banging on the door for several minutes. The big dark one with an elaborate moustache held out in a hand wearing a plaited gilt ring some sort of identity card.

Dr von Leinsdorf said quietly, the blood coming strangely back to legs and arms, "What is it?"

9 **(to hold s.o.) at bay:** jdn. in Schach halten.
16 **to unslot:** öffnen, lösen.
to loop: schlingen, winden.
17 **serrated:** gezackt.
knob: Knopf, Knauf.
Yale lock: Sicherheitsschloß.
20 f. **elaborate:** gepflegt.
21 **plaited:** geflochten.
gilt (auch: *gilded*): vergoldet, golden.

The sergeant told him they knew there was a coloured girl in the flat. They had had information; "I been watching this flat three month, I know."

"I am alone here." Dr von Leinsdorf did not raise his voice.

"I know, I know who is here. Come –" And the sergeant and his two assistants went into the living-room, the kitchen, the bath-room (the sergeant picked up a bottle of after-shave cologne, seemed to study the French label) and the bedroom. The assistants removed the clean laundry that was laid upon the bed and then turned back the bedding, carrying the sheets over to be examined by the sergeant under the lamp. They talked to one another in Afrikaans, which the Doctor did not understand. The sergeant himself looked under the bed, and lifted the long curtains at the window. The wall cupboard was of the kind that has no knobs; he saw that it was locked and began to ask in Afrikaans, then politely changed to English, "Give us the key."

Dr von Leinsdorf said, "I'm sorry, I left it at my office – I always lock and take my keys with me in the mornings."

"It's no good, man, you better give me the key."

He smiled a little, reasonably. "It's on my office desk."

The assistants produced a screwdriver and he watched while they inserted it where the cupboard doors met, gave it quick, firm but not forceful leverage. He heard the lock give.

She had been naked, it was true, when they knocked. But

25 **screwdriver:** Schraubenzieher.
26 **to insert:** einsetzen, einführen.
27 **leverage:** Hebelkraft.

now she was wearing a long-sleeved T-shirt with an appliquéd butterfly motif on one breast, and a pair of jeans. Her feet were still bare; she had managed, by feel, in the dark, to get into some of the clothing she had snatched from the bed, but she had no shoes. She had perhaps been weeping behind the cupboard door (her cheeks looked stained) but now her face was sullen and she was breathing heavily, her diaphragm contracting and expanding exaggeratedly and her breasts pushing against the cloth. It made her appear angry; it might simply have been that she was half-suffocated in the cupboard and needed oxygen. She did not look at Dr von Leinsdorf. She would not reply to the sergeant's questions.

They were taken to the police station where they were at once separated and in turn led for examination by the district surgeon. The man's underwear was taken away and examined, as the sheets had been, for signs of his seed. When the girl was undressed, it was discovered that beneath her jeans she was wearing a pair of men's briefs with his name on the neatly-sewn laundry tag; in her haste, she had taken the wrong garment to her hiding-place.

Now she cried, standing there before the district surgeon in a man's underwear.

1 f. **appliquéd:** aus anderem Stoff aufgenäht.
7 **sullen:** finster, düster, mürrisch.
8 **diaphragm:** Zwerchfell.
9 **exaggeratedly** (adv.): übertrieben.
11 **half-suffocated:** halb erstickt.
12 **oxygen:** Sauerstoff.
16 **district surgeon:** Bezirksarzt.
19 **briefs** (pl.): Unterhose, Slip.
20 **laundry tag:** Wäschezeichen.

He courteously pretended not to notice. He handed briefs, jeans and T-shirt round the door, and motioned her to lie on a white-sheeted high table where he placed her legs apart, resting in stirrups, and put into her where the other had made his way so warmly a cold hard instrument that expanded wider and wider. Her thighs and knees trembled uncontrollably while the doctor looked into her and touched her deep inside with more hard instruments, carrying wafers of gauze.

When she came out of the examining room back to the charge office, Dr von Leinsdorf was not there; they must have taken him somewhere else. She spent what was left of the night in a cell, as he must be doing; but early in the morning she was released and taken home to her mother's house in the coloured township by a white man who explained he was the clerk of the lawyer who had been engaged for her by Dr von Leinsdorf. Dr von Leinsdorf, the clerk said, had also been bailed out that morning. He did not say when, or if she would see him again.

A statement made by the girl to the police was handed in to Court when she and the man appeared to meet charges of contravening the Immorality Act in a Johannesburg flat on the night of – December, 19–. *I lived with the white man in his flat. He had intercourse with me sometimes. He*

1 **courteously** (adv.): höflich, zuvorkommend.
2 **to motion:** (mit Gesten) anweisen.
4 **stirrup:** Steigbügel.
9 **wafer:** dünne Schicht, Lage.
gauze: Gaze, Mull.
11 **charge office:** Anklage-Büro.
18 **to bail out:** gegen Kaution freilassen.
22 **to contravene s.th.:** gegen etwas verstoßen.
24 **intercourse:** Geschlechtsverkehr.

gave me tablets to take to prevent me becoming pregnant.

Interviewed by the Sunday papers, the girl said, "I'm sorry for the sadness brought to my mother." She said she was one of nine children of a female laundry worker. She had left school in Standard Three because there was no money at home for gym clothes or a school blazer. She had worked as a machinist in a factory and a cashier in a supermarket. Dr von Leinsdorf taught her to type his notes.

Dr Franz-Josef von Leinsdorf, described as the grandson of a baroness, a cultured man engaged in international mineralogical research, said he accepted social distinctions between people but didn't think they should be legally imposed. "Even in my own country it's difficult for a person from a higher class to marry one from a lower class."

The two accused gave no evidence. They did not greet or speak to each other in Court. The Defence argued that the sergeant's evidence that they had been living together as man and wife was hearsay. (The woman with the dachshund, the caretaker?) The magistrate acquitted them because the State failed to prove carnal intercourse had taken place on the night of – December, 19–.

1 f. **pregnant:** schwanger.
6 **Standard Three:** letztes Jahr der Grundschule (in Südafrika).
7 **gym clothes** (pl.): Turnkleidung.
school blazer: Jacke der Schuluniform.
12 **cultured:** kultiviert.
13 f. **distinctions:** Unterschiede.
15 **to impose:** auferlegen, verhängen, aufzwingen.
22 **magistrate:** Amtsrichter.
to acquit: freisprechen.
23 **carnal:** fleischlich, körperlich.

The girl's mother was quoted, with photograph, in the Sunday papers: "I won't let my daughter work as a servant for a white man again."

Two

The farm children play together when they are small; but once the white children go away to school they soon don't play together any more, even in the holidays. Although most of the black children get some sort of schooling, they drop every year farther behind the grades passed by the white children; the childish vocabulary, the child's exploration of the adventurous possibilities of dam, koppies, mealie lands and veld – there comes a time when the white children have surpassed these with the vocabulary of boarding-school and the possibilities of inter-school sports matches and the kind of adventures seen at the cinema. This usefully coincides with the age of twelve or thirteen; so that by the time early adolescence is reached, the black children are making, along with the bodily changes common to all, an easy transition to adult forms of address, beginning to call their old playmates *missus* and *baasie* – little master.

1 **to quote:** anführen, zitieren.
11 f. **koppies** (Afrik.): kleinere Hügel, Bergland.
12 **mealie lands** (S.Afr.): Maisfelder.
14 **boarding-school:** Internatsschule.
16 **to coincide:** zusammentreffen.
17 **adolescence:** Jugend, Pubertät.
19 **transition:** Übergang.
21 **baasie** (Afrik.): Sohn des Hausherrn, junger Herr (Diminutiv von *baas* ›Herr‹).

The trouble was Paulus Eysendyck did not seem to realize that Thebedi was now simply one of the crowd of farm children down at the kraal, recognizable in his sisters' old clothes. The first Christmas holidays after he had gone to boarding-school he brought home for Thebedi a painted box he made in his wood-work class. He had to give it to her secretly because he had nothing for the other children at the kraal. And she gave him, before he went back to school, a bracelet she had made of thin brass wire and the grey-and-white beans of the castor-oil crop his father cultivated. (When they used to play together, she was the one who had taught Paulus how to make clay oxen for their toy spans.) There was a craze, even in the *platteland* towns like the one where he was at school, for boys to wear elephant-hair and other bracelets beside their watch-straps; his was admired, friends asked him to get similar ones for them. He said the natives made them on his father's farm and he would try.

When he was fifteen, six feet tall, and tramping round at school dances with the girls from the "sister" school in the same town; when he had learnt how to tease and flirt and fondle quite intimately these girls who were the daughters of prosperous farmers like his father; when he

3 **kraal:** südafrikanisches Hüttendorf.
9 **bracelet:** Armband.
10f. **castor-oil crop:** Rizinusölernte.
13 **span** (S.Afr.): (Ochsen-, Pferde-)Gespann.
craze: Masche, Mode.
14 **platteland** (Afrik.): Land, ländliche Gegend.
16 **watch-strap:** Uhrarmband.
20 **to tramp:** stapfen, stampfen.
22 **to tease:** necken, hänseln.
23 **to fondle:** streicheln, tätscheln.

had even met one who, at a wedding he had attended with his parents on a nearby farm, had let him do with her in a locked storeroom what people did when they made love – when he was as far from his childhood as all this, he still brought home from a shop in town a red plastic belt and gilt hoop ear-rings for the black girl, Thebedi. She told her father the missus had given these to her as a reward for some work she had done – it was true she sometimes was called to help out in the farmhouse. She told the girls in the kraal that she had a sweetheart nobody knew about, far away, away on another farm, and they giggled, and teased, and admired her. There was a boy in the kraal called Njabulo who said he wished he could have bought her a belt and ear-rings.

When the farmer's son was home for the holidays she wandered far from the kraal and her companions. He went for walks alone. They had not arranged this; it was an urge each followed independently. He knew it was she, from a long way off. She knew that his dog would not bark at her. Down at the dried-up river-bed where five or six years ago the children had caught a leguaan one great day – a creature that combined ideally the size and ferocious aspect of the crocodile with the harmlessness of the lizard – they squatted side by side on the earth bank. He told her traveller's tales: about school, about the punishments at school, particularly, exaggerating both their nature and his indifference to them. He told her about the town of Middleburg, which she had never seen. She

3 **storeroom:** Lagerraum, Speicher.
6 **hoop:** Reifen, Ring.
22 f. **ferocious:** wild, grimmig.
24 **lizard:** Eidechse.
to squat: kauern, hocken.

had nothing to tell but she prompted with many questions, like any good listener. While he talked he twisted and tugged at the roots of white stinkwood and Cape willow trees that looped out of the eroded earth around them. It had always been a good spot for children's games, down there hidden by the mesh of old, ant-eaten trees held in place by vigorous ones, wild asparagus bushing up between the trunks, and here and there prickly-pear cactus sunken-skinned and bristly, like an old man's face, keeping alive sapless until the next rainy season. She punctured the dry hide of a prickly-pear again and again with a sharp stick while she listened. She laughed a lot at what he told her, sometimes dropping her face on her knees, sharing amusement with the cool shady earth beneath her bare feet. She put on her pair of shoes – white sandals thickly Blanco-ed against the farm dust – when he was on the farm, but these were taken off and laid aside, at the river-bed.

One summer afternoon when there was water flowing there and it was very hot she waded in as they used to do

1 **to prompt:** nachhelfen, weiterdrängen.
3 **to tug:** ziehen, zerren.
stinkwood: teures, teakähnliches, südafrikanisches Holz.
3f. **Cape willow trees:** Weiden, wie sie in der Gegend um das Kap der Guten Hoffnung wachsen.
4 **to erode:** auswaschen, zersetzen.
6 **mesh:** hier: Wurzelwerk.
ant-eaten: von Ameisen zerfressen.
7 **asparagus:** Spargel.
8f. **prickly-pear cactus:** Feigenkaktus.
9 **bristly:** stachlig.
10 **sapless:** ohne Saft, saftlos.
11 **to puncture:** durchlöchern.
hide: Haut, Schale.
16 **Blanco-ed:** mit weißer Schuhcreme bestrichen.

when they were children, her dress bunched modestly and tucked into the legs of her pants. The schoolgirls he went swimming with at dams or pools on neighbouring farms wore bikinis but the sight of their dazzling bellies and thighs in the sunlight had never made him feel what he felt now, when the girl came up the bank and sat beside him, the drops of water beading off her dark legs the only points of light in the earth-smelling, deep shade. They were not afraid of one another, they had known one another always; he did with her what he had done that time in the storeroom at the wedding, and this time it was so lovely, so lovely, he was surprised . . . and she was surprised by it, too – he could see in her dark face that was part of the shade, with her big dark eyes, shiny as soft water, watching him attentively: as she had when they used to huddle over their teams of mud oxen, as she had when he told her about detention weekends at school.

They went to the river-bed often through those summer holidays. They met just before the light went, as it does quite quickly, and each returned home with the dark – she to her mother's hut, he to the farmhouse – in time for the evening meal. He did not tell her about school or town any more. She did not ask questions any longer. He told her, each time, when they would meet again. Once

1 **bunched:** gebündelt, gerafft.
2 **to tuck:** schürzen, aufkrempeln, in Falten legen.
4 **to dazzle:** blenden, verwirren.
belly: Bauch, Leib.
5 **thigh:** Oberschenkel.
7 **to bead:** perlen.
16 **to huddle:** sich zusammenkuscheln.
17 **detention weekend:** Nachsitzen an einem Wochenende.

or twice it was very early in the morning; the lowing of the cows being driven to graze came to them where they lay, dividing them with unspoken recognition of the sound read in their two pairs of eyes, opening so close to each other.

He was a popular boy at school. He was in the second, then the first soccer team. The head girl of the "sister" school was said to have a crush on him; he didn't particularly like her, but there was a pretty blonde who put up her long hair into a kind of doughnut with a black ribbon round it, whom he took to see films when the schoolboys and girls had a free Saturday afternoon. He had been driving tractors and other farm vehicles since he was ten years old, and as soon as he was eighteen he got a driver's licence and in the holidays, this last year of his school life, he took neighbours' daughters to dances and to the drive-in cinema that had just opened twenty kilometres from the farm. His sisters were married, by then; his parents often left him in charge of the farm over the weekend while they visited the young wives and grandchildren.

When Thebedi saw the farmer and his wife drive away on a Saturday afternoon, the boot of their Mercedes filled with fresh-killed poultry and vegetables from the garden that it was part of her father's work to tend, she knew that

1 **to low:** muhen.
2 **to graze:** grasen, weiden.
7 **soccer:** Fußball.
8 **to have a crush on s.o.:** für jdn. schwärmen.
10 **doughnut:** (Berliner) Pfannkuchen, Krapfen.
19 **charge:** Obhut, Verantwortung.
22 **boot:** Kofferraum.
23 **poultry:** Geflügel.
24 **to tend:** pflegen.

she must come not to the river-bed but up to the house. The house was an old one, thick-walled, dark against the heat. The kitchen was its lively thoroughfare, with servants, food supplies, begging cats and dogs, pots boiling over, washing being damped for ironing, and the big deep-freeze the missus had ordered from town, bearing a crocheted mat and a vase of plastic irises. But the dining-room with the bulging-legged heavy table was shut up in its rich, old smell of soup and tomato sauce. The sitting-room curtains were drawn and the T.V. set silent. The door of the parents' bedroom was locked and the empty rooms where the girls had slept had sheets of plastic spread over the beds. It was in one of these that she and the farmer's son stayed together whole nights – almost: she had to get away before the house servants, who knew her, came in at dawn. There was a risk someone would discover her or traces of her presence if he took her to his own bedroom, although she had looked into it many times when she was helping out in the house and knew well, there, the row of silver cups he had won at school.

When she was eighteen and the farmer's son nineteen and working with his father on the farm before entering a veterinary college, the young man Njabulo asked her father for her. Njabulo's parents met with hers and the money he was to pay in place of the cows it is customary to give a prospective bride's parents was settled upon. He had no cows to offer; he was a labourer on the Eysendyck

3 **thoroughfare:** (Haupt-)Verkehrsstraße.
7 **chrocheted:** gehäkelt, Häkel-.
8 **bulging-legged:** mit bauchigen (Tisch-)Beinen.
24 **veterinary college:** Tierärztliche Hochschule.
27 **prospective:** zukünftig.

farm, like her father. A bright youngster; old Eysendyck had taught him brick-laying and was using him for odd jobs in construction, around the place. She did not tell the farmer's son that her parents had arranged for her to marry. She did not tell him, either, before he left for his first term at the veterinary college, that she thought she was going to have a baby. Two months after her marriage to Njabulo, she gave birth to a daughter. There was no disgrace in that; among her people it is customary for a young man to make sure, before marriage, that the chosen girl is not barren, and Njabulo had made love to her then. But the infant was very light and did not quickly grow darker as most African babies do. Already at birth there was on its head a quantity of straight, fine floss, like that which carries the seeds of certain weeds in the veld. The unfocused eyes it opened were grey flecked with yellow. Njabulo was the matt, opaque coffee-grounds colour that has always been called black; the colour of Thebedi's legs on which beaded water looked oyster-shell blue, the same colour as Thebedi's face, where the black eyes, with their interested gaze and clear whites, were so dominant.

Njabulo made no complaint. Out of his farm labourer's earnings he bought from the Indian store a cellophane-windowed pack containing a pink plastic bath, six napkins, a card of safety pins, a knitted jacket, cap and

1 **youngster:** Junge.
11 **barren:** unfruchtbar.
12 **infant:** (Klein-)Kind.
14 **floss:** Flaum.
16 **unfocused:** mit leerem Blick.
17 **opaque:** trübe.
25 f. **napkin:** Windel.

bootees, a dress, and a tin of Johnson's Baby Powder, for Thebedi's baby.

When it was two weeks old Paulus Eysendyck arrived home from the veterinary college for the holidays. He drank a glass of fresh, still-warm milk in the childhood familiarity of his mother's kitchen and heard her discussing with the old house-servant where they could get a reliable substitute to help out now that the girl Thebedi had had a baby. For the first time since he was a small boy he came right into the kraal. It was eleven o'clock in the morning. The men were at work in the lands. He looked about him, urgently; the women turned away, each not wanting to be the one approached to point out where Thebedi lived. Thebedi appeared, coming slowly from the hut Njabulo had built in white man's style, with a tin chimney, and a proper window with glass panes set in straight as walls made of unfired bricks would allow. She greeted him with hands brought together and a token movement representing the respectful bob with which she was accustomed to acknowledge she was in the presence of his father or mother. He lowered his head under the doorway of her home and went in. He said, "I want to see. Show me."

She had taken the bundle off her back before she came out into the light to face him. She moved between the iron bedstead made up with Njabulo's checked blankets

1 **bootees:** gestrickte Babyschuhe.
17 **panes:** Fensterscheiben.
18 **unfired bricks:** ungebrannte Ziegel.
19 **token:** Zeichen, Symbol.
20 **bob:** Verbeugung, Auf- und Niederbewegung des Kopfes.
27 **checked:** kariert.

and the small wooden table where the pink plastic bath stood among food and kitchen pots, and picked up the bundle from the snugly-blanketed grocer's box where it lay. The infant was asleep; she revealed the closed, pale, plump tiny face, with a bubble of spit at the corner of the mouth, the spidery pink hands stirring. She took off the woollen cap and the straight fine hair flew up after it in static electricity, showing gilded strands here and there. He said nothing. She was watching him as she had done when they were little, and the gang of children had trodden down a crop in their games or transgressed in some other way for which he, as the farmer's son, the white one among them, must intercede with the farmer. She disturbed the sleeping face by scratching or tickling gently at a cheek with one finger, and slowly the eyes opened, saw nothing, were still asleep, and then, awake, no longer narrowed, looked out at them, grey with yellowish flecks, his own hazel eyes.

He struggled for a moment with a grimace of tears, anger and self-pity. She could not put out her hand to him. He said, "You haven't been near the house with it?"

She shook her head.

"Never?"

Again she shook her head.

3 **snugly-blanketed:** behaglich zugedeckt.
5 **spit:** Speichel, Spucke.
6 **spidery:** spinnenähnlich.
8 **strand:** Strähne.
10 **gang:** Horde.
11 **to transgress:** sich vergehen, fehlen.
13 **to intercede with s.o.:** sich bei jdm. einsetzen, bei jdm. Fürsprache einlegen.
18 **hazel:** haselnußbraun.

"Don't take it out. Stay inside. Can't you take it away somewhere. You must give it to someone –"

She moved to the door with him.

He said, "I'll see what I will do. I don't know." And then he said: "I feel like killing myself."

Her eyes began to glow, to thicken with tears. For a moment there was the feeling between them that used to come when they were alone down at the river-bed.

He walked out.

Two days later, when his mother and father had left the farm for the day, he appeared again. The women were away on the lands, weeding, as they were employed to do as casual labour in summer; only the very old remained, propped up on the ground outside the huts in the flies and the sun.Thebedi did not ask him in. The child had not been well; it had diarrhoea. He asked where its food was. She said, "The milk comes from me." He went into Njabulo's house, where the child lay; she did not follow but stayed outside the door and watched without seeing an old crone who had lost her mind, talking to herself, talking to the fowls who ignored her.

She thought she heard small grunts from the hut, the kind of infant grunt that indicates a full stomach, a deep sleep. After a time, long or short she did not know, he came out and walked away with plodding stride (his father's gait) out of sight, towards his father's house.

13 **casual labour:** Aushilfsarbeit.
14 **to prop up:** sich lehnen, stützen.
16 **diarrhoea:** Durchfall.
20 **crone:** alte Frau, Hexe.
21 **fowl:** Geflügel, Huhn.
22 **grunt:** Grunzen.
25 **to plod:** einherstapfen.
gait: Gang, Schreiten.

The baby was not fed during the night and although she kept telling Njabulo it was sleeping, he saw for himself in the morning that it was dead. He comforted her with words and caresses. She did not cry but simply sat, staring at the door. Her hands were cold as dead chickens' feet to his touch.

Njabulo buried the little baby where farm workers were buried, in the place in the veld the farmer had given them. Some of the mounds had been left to weather away unmarked, others were covered with stones and a few had fallen wooden crosses. He was going to make a cross but before it was finished the police came and dug up the grave and took away the dead baby: someone – one of the other labourers? their women? – had reported that the baby was almost white, that, strong and healthy, it had died suddenly after a visit by the farmer's son. Pathological tests on the infant corpse showed intestinal damage not always consistent with death by natural causes.

Thebedi went for the first time to the country town where Paulus had been to school, to give evidence at the preparatory examination into the charge of murder brought against him. She cried hysterically in the witness box, saying yes, yes (the gilt hoop ear-rings swung in her ears),

4 **caress:** Liebkosung, Streicheln.
9 **mound:** Hügel, Wall.
to weather away: verwittern.
17 **pathological:** pathologisch, krankhaft.
corpse: Leichnam, Leiche.
17 f. **intestinal:** Darm-.
18 **consistent:** übereinstimmend.
21 f. **preparatory examination:** vorbereitendes Verhör, Vorverhör.
22 **charge:** Anklage.

she saw the accused pouring liquid into the baby's mouth. She said he had threatened to shoot her if she told anyone.

More than a year went by before, in that same town, the case was brought to trial. She came to Court with a new-born baby on her back. She wore gilt hoop ear-rings; she was calm; she said she had not seen what the white man did in the house.

Paulus Eysendyck said he had visited the hut but had not poisoned the child.

The Defence did not contest that there had been a love relationship between the accused and the girl, or that intercourse had taken place, but submitted there was no proof that the child was the accused's.

The judge told the accused there was strong suspicion against him but not enough proof that he had committed the crime. The Court could not accept the girl's evidence because it was clear she had committed perjury either at this trial or at the preparatory examination. There was the suggestion in the mind of the Court that she might be an accomplice in the crime; but, again, insufficient proof.

The judge commended the honourable behaviour of the husband (sitting in court in a brown-and-yellow-quartered golf cap bought for Sundays) who had not rejected his wife and had "even provided clothes for the unfortunate infant out of his slender means".

11 **to contest:** anfechten.
13 **to submit:** zu Bedenken geben.
18 **perjury:** Meineid.
21 **accomplice:** Komplize.
23 **to commend:** empfehlen, loben.
25 **to reject:** verwerfen, ablehnen.
27 **slender means:** bescheidene finanzielle Mittel.

The verdict on the accused was "not guilty".
The young white man refused to accept the congratulations of press and public and left the Court with his mother's raincoat shielding his face from photographers. His father said to the press, "I will try and carry on as best I can to hold up my head in the district."
Interviewed by the Sunday papers, who spelled her name in a variety of ways, the black girl, speaking in her own language, was quoted beneath her photograph: "It was a thing of our childhood, we don't see each other any more."

1 **verdict:** Urteilsspruch.

Editorische Notiz

Der englische Text folgt den Ausgaben: Nadine Gordimer, *Selected Stories*, Harmondsworth: Penguin, 1986 (*Some Monday For Sure*, *Which New Era Would That Be?*), und: Nadine Gordimer, *A Soldier's Embrace. Stories*, Harmondsworth: Penguin, 1985 (*Town and Country Lovers*). Das Glossar erklärt in der Regel alle Wörter, die über die Wertigkeitsstufe 4 des *Englischen Arbeitswörterbuches* von Alfred Haase (Frankfurt a. M.: Moritz Diesterweg, [7]1979) hinausgehen. Im Zweifelsfall wurde großzügig verfahren, d. h. eher eine Vokabel mehr aufgenommen als dort vorgesehen. – Die einzelnen Erzählungen sind unabhängig voneinander glossiert.

Im Glossar verwendete Abkürzungen

adv.	adverb
Afrik.	Afrikaans
arab.	arabisch
fig.	figuratively (übertragen)
Fr.	French
Lat.	Latin
o.s.	oneself
pl.	plural
S. Afr.	South African
s.o.	someone
s.th.	something

Literaturhinweise

Bibliographien

Racilia J. Nell, *Nadine Gordimer: Novelist and Short Story Writer. A Bibliography of Her Works and Selected Literary Criticism*, Johannesburg 1964.

William H. New, »Nadine Gordimer«, in: W. H. N., *Critical Writings on Commonwealth Literature: A Selective Bibliography to 1975*, London 1975, S. 219 f.

John Cooke, »Nadine Gordimer. A Bibliography«, in: *Bulletin of Bibliography and Magazine Notes* 36 (1979) S. 81–84.

Sekundärliteratur

Alan Ross, »A Writer in South Africa: Nadine Gordimer«, in: *London Magazine* 5 (1965), Nr. 2, S. 21–28.

Robert F. Haugh, *Nadine Gordimer*, New York 1974.

Kevin Magarey, »Cutting the Jewel: Facets of Art in Nadine Gordimer's Short Stories«, in: *Southern Review*, Adelaide, 7 (1974) S. 3–28.

Robert J. Green, »Nadine Gordimer: The Politics of Race«, in: *World Literature Written in English* 16 (1977) S. 256–262.

Elizabeth Gerver, »Women Revolutionaries in the Novels of Nadine Gordimer and Doris Lessing«, in: *World Literature Written in English* 17 (1978) S. 38–50.

Michael Wade, *Nadine Gordimer*, London 1978.

C. P. Sarvan, *Aspects of Freedom in Southern African Fiction. A Study of the Works of Nadine Gordimer*, Diss. London 1979.

Irene Wettenhall, »Liberalism and Radicalism in South Africa since 1948: Nadine Gordimer's Fiction«, in: *New Literature Review* 8 (1980) S. 36–44.

Dorian Haarhoff, »Two Cheers for Socialism: Nadine Gordimer and E. M. Forster«, in: *English in Africa* 7 (1980) S. 55–64.

Stephen Clingman, »History of the Inside: The Novels of Nadine Gordimer«, in: *Journal of Southern African Studies* 7 (1981) S. 165–193.

Stephen Gray, »Interview with Nadine Gordimer«, in: *Contemporary Literature* 22 (1981) S. 263–271.

John W. Cooke, »Out of the Garden: Nadine Gordimer's Novels«, in: *Design and Intent in African Literature*, hrsg. von David F. Dorsey, Washington 1982, S. 17–27.

Paul Rich, »Tradition and Revolt in South African Fiction: The Novels of André Brink, Nadine Gordimer and J. M. Coetzee«, in: *Journal of Southern African Studies* 8 (1982) S. 54 bis 93.

Dorothy Driver, »Nadine Gordimer: The Politicization of Women«, in: *English in Africa* 10 (1983) S. 29–54.

Christopher Heywood, *Nadine Gordimer*, London 1983.

Robert Boyers, »A Conversation with Nadine Gordimer«, in: *Salmagundi* 62 (1984) S. 3–31.

Stephen Clingman, »Multi-Racialism or A World of Strangers«, in: *Salmagundi* 62 (1984) S. 32–61.

Christiane Degen, *Gesellschaftskritik im anglophonen Gegenwartsroman Afrikas*, Frankfurt a. M. 1984.

Paul Rich, »Apartheid and the Decline of the Civilization Idea«, in: *Research in African Literatures* 15 (1984) S. 365 bis 393.

Stephen Clingman, *The Novels of Nadine Gordimer*, London 1986.

Nachwort

Seit Jahrzehnten schreibt Nadine Gordimer noble und feinfühlige Geschichten und Romane über ein einziges Thema: das Apartheid-Regime in ihrer Heimat Südafrika (das inzwischen länger andauert als das »Tausendjährige Reich« in Deutschland). Sie hat mit ihren Büchern Anerkennung, Respekt, ja Bewunderung in aller Welt gefunden und ist heute, zusammen mit Doris Lessing und V. S. Naipaul, preisüberhäuft und in viele Sprachen übersetzt, eine der großen Figuren der Commonwealth-Literatur. Nadine Gordimer ist von dem Drang getrieben, ihr Leiden an der Ungerechtigkeit der Rassentrennung in Geschichten auszudrücken – Geschichten, die das »weiße Gewissen« Südafrikas ebenso wie die hochentwickelten literarischen Darstellungsmöglichkeiten einer europäisch geprägten Intellektuellen widerspiegeln. Geboren wurde sie am 20. November 1923 in Springs – damals eine kleine Bergarbeiterstadt in Witwatersrand, der Goldgrube Südafrikas, heute ein Vorort von Johannesburg. Der Vater Isidor war ein russischer Jude, Uhrmacher von Beruf, die Mutter Engländerin. Schon auf der Klosterschule in Johannesburg begann sie zu schreiben, intensiver dann während des Anglistikstudiums an der University of Witwatersrand: Gedichte, Kurzgeschichten, gefärbt von gieriger Klassiker-Lektüre, Kostproben eines ungewöhnlichen Artikulationstalents und hochgradiger Empfindlichkeit. »Aufwachsen in einer südafrikanischen Goldminenstadt als Angehörige einer weißen Minderheit – das bedeutete die totale Isolierung als Intellektuelle; ich wußte nicht einmal, daß ich eine war. Der Begriff der Intellektualität, den ich aus Büchern kannte, gehörte so entschieden in die nördliche Hemisphäre wie eine weiße Weihnacht. In jener Kleinstadt, die zwischen Bergwerkshalden eingepfercht war, lebte ich wie im Exil von der europäischen Geisteswelt und wußte nicht einmal, daß eine solche Welt auch unter Afrikanern existierte.«[1] Die Englisch schreibenden

1 Nadine Gordimer, *Leben im Interregnum. Essays zu Politik und Literatur*, Frankfurt a. M. 1987, S. 46.

Schriftsteller in Südafrika sahen sich seit den Tagen von Olive Schreiner (1855–1920), der Begründerin der südafrikanischen Literatur, in der Rolle von Chronisten und Kritikern ihres sozialen Umfeldes; geprägt vom europäischen Realismus des 19. Jahrhunderts hatten Autoren wie Roy Campbell, William Plomer, Laurens van der Post und Alan Paton eine robuste literarische Tradition begründet, in die sich Nadine Gordimer zunächst willig einordnete. »Ich schrieb, bevor ich wußte, was Politik bedeutet – ich schrieb, um das Geheimnis des Lebens zu verstehen«,[2] hat sie später über diese Zeit gesagt. *Come Again Tomorrow* hieß ihre erste veröffentlichte Kurzgeschichte – Nadine Gordimer war fünfzehn, als dieser Text 1939 in der Zeitschrift *Forum* erschien. Seither hat sie hartnäckig an der Einsicht festgehalten, daß die Kunst des Schriftstellers gerade darin besteht, sich in a n d e r e Menschen zu versetzen – nicht in sich selbst. Die anderen Menschen: das sind für Nadine Gordimer die Bewohner Südafrikas, Schwarze wie Weiße. Als »Fremde unter Fremden« – so heißt einer ihrer frühen Romane (*A World of Strangers*) – hat sie sich rückhaltlos den Problemen dieses Landes verschrieben (und in Südafrika auch ihren ständigen Wohnsitz behalten).

Die formale Tradition, in der sie sich bewegt, ist die europäisch-amerikanische realistische Erzählkonvention, aber die Themen liefert ihr das post-koloniale Afrika, in dem sich Weiße und Schwarze gleichermaßen gefangen und bedroht fühlen; die Weißen gequält von Zweifeln an der Berechtigung der eigenen Machtpositionen, die Schwarzen in der Phase revolutionärer Selbstbesinnung. »Nicht ein jugendlicher Ausflug in die Kommunistische Partei hat mir die Augen für die Afrikaner und die Schädlichkeit der Rassenschranken geöffnet, sondern die scheinbar so esoterische Höhlenforschung des Zweifels – unter der Führung von Kafka, und nicht von Marx. Die ›Probleme‹ meines Landes brachten mich nicht zum Schreiben. Im Gegenteil: ich lernte schreiben, und das ließ mich durch die Oberflä-

2 Renate Schostack, »Leiden am Rassenwahn. Gespräch mit der südafrikanischen Schriftstellerin Nadine Gordimer«, in: *Frankfurter Allgemeine Zeitung*, 9. Oktober 1982, S. 23.

che des südafrikanischen Lebens fallen und fallen ...«[3] In den ersten Romanen (*The Lying Days*, 1953; *A World of Strangers*, 1958; *Occasion for Loving*, 1963) geht es in der einen oder anderen Form immer um die Frage »Where Do Whites Fit In?« (so der Titel eines Essays aus dem Jahre 1959). Was sollen die Weißen in Südafrika tun – dableiben, oder das Land verlassen? Die Tendenz ist jetzt noch: lieber bleiben, zu helfen versuchen, denn die Weißen sind, nach Nadine Gordimer, »Repräsentanten von technischen, wissenschaftlichen und kulturellen Errungenschaften, die sie viele Jahrhunderte vor der schwarzen Zivilisation erworben haben.«[4] Eine solche Einstellung wird etwa zur gleichen Zeit von Autoren wie Wole Soyinka oder James Ngugi zunehmend in Zweifel gezogen: das Modell der industriellen Expansion, wie es das Europa des 19. Jahrhunderts geliefert hatte, erweist sich in Südafrika als nicht anwendbar. Nadine Gordimer gewinnt allmählich Distanz zu jener *Late Bourgeois World*, von der sie in dem gleichnamigen Roman (1966) berichtet. Das Scheitern des politischen Liberalismus im Gefolge des Verbots des National Congress führt zu komplizierten Veränderungen in der Psyche der weißen Südafrikaner: man fühlt sich nicht mehr in der Rolle von Pionieren auf vorgeschobenem Posten – Typen, wie sie in den Romanen von J. F. Cooper verherrlicht worden waren –, sondern als Opfer von sozialen und rassischen Spannungen, die unausweichlich in die Tragödie führen. Einzig die Figur des politischen Einzelkämpfers nimmt eine Ausnahmestellung ein. Ein »Ehrengast« (*A Guest of Honour*, 1971; dt. 1986) wie Evelyn Bray – Ehrengast in einer fiktiven zentralafrikanischen Republik, die er aus kolonialer Unterdrückung errichten half – illustriert die resignierende Einsicht, daß das Erreichen revolutionärer Ziele in der Regel auch das Ende der Freiheit bedeutet. Soll Afrika seine Identität in der Imitation europäisch-abendländischer Vorbilder finden? Oder soll sich das Land ein für allemal von seinen ungebetenen ausländischen Helfern befreien? Nadine Gordi-

3 *Leben im Interregnum*, S. 58.
4 *Dialog. Helmut Winter im Gespräch mit Nadine Gordimer*, Hessischer Rundfunk, 2. Programm, 11. Januar 1987.

mer gibt keine eindeutigen Antworten, bietet keine Lösungen an; sie dringt statt dessen tiefer ein in die Probleme ethnischer und kultureller Eigenständigkeit, schreibt Aufsätze und Bücher über die schwarze Literatur und spürt einer Tradition nach, die sie verschüttet, nicht erloschen wähnt. Die Erneuerung Südafrikas, so meint sie in *The Conservationist* (1974), kann nur aus der verborgenen Kraft der »Verdammten dieser Erde« selbst kommen, aus den Reserven der schwarzen Bevölkerung, die, was ihr genommen wurde, eines Tages wieder besitzen wird. Wie ein Land unter der Last einer räuberischen Industrialisierung erstickt, wie sich eine Gesellschaft in selbstzerstörerischer Aggressivität zersetzt, wie aber zugleich menschlich-kreatürliche Instinkte und die Regenerationskraft einer unerschöpflichen Natur dem Persönlichkeitsverfall, der Hoffnungslosigkeit und Anonymität entgegenwirken – damit beschäftigen sich die Romane und Erzählungen der Nadine Gordimer aus den siebziger Jahren.

Im Kern getroffen von den Soweto-Aufständen (1976), entwirft sie in *Burger's Daughter* (1979) das Porträt einer selbstbewußten, eigenwilligen Frau, die den Weg zu aktivem politischem Widerstand findet, in *July's People* (1981) ein Panorama des nach-revolutionären Lebens einer urbanen Familie mit Afrikaner-Hintergrund. Ähnlich wie in Doris Lessings *The Grass is Singing* geht es hier um Verwandlungen, um den Übergang von einer Kultur in die andere, aber ohne die Gewißheit der Reintegration. Stärker als früher verwendet Nadine Gordimer in dieser Phase mythische Stoffe und Erzählstrukturen – überzeugt davon, daß sich Weiße und Schwarze auf symbolischer Ebene ohnehin berühren: »Wir, die Weißen und die Schwarzen, sind seit 350 Jahren trotz aller Gesetze fest miteinander verbunden. Es gibt Lebensbereiche, in denen wir einander nicht täuschen können, in denen wir uns blind verstehen, weil wir zwischen den Zeilen lesen.«[5]

Wie die großen russischen Schriftsteller des 19. Jahrhunderts ist sie von der Vorstellung durchdrungen, daß die Gesellschaft,

5 Ebd.

deren Kind sie ist, nicht nur – wie jede Gesellschaft – überaus unvollkommen organisiert ist, sondern in skandalösem Widerspruch zu jenen Prinzipien handelt, als deren Vertreterin sie sich scheinheilig aufspielt. Diese Überzeugung ist der Grundton ihrer Werke und färbt auf alles ab, was sie beschreibt: afrikanische Gerüche, Farben und Geschmackseindrücke, die Häuser und Straßen, Landschaften und Siedlungen, die ihren Lesern inzwischen so vertraut sind. Nadine Gordimer ist keine moralisierende, didaktisch orientierte Autorin, in ihren Geschichten gibt es weder beißende Satire noch apokalyptische Stimmungen, und trotzdem hat sie etwas von einer Seherin. *A Sport of Nature* (1987) zum Beispiel ist der Versuch, über die Konstellation von Furcht und Schrecken in Südafrika hinaus in die Zukunft zu blicken, auf einen Kontinent, in dem die Schwarzen sich selbst regieren. Eine solche Perspektive bedingt emphatischeres Erzählen, führt zu ungeduldigem Verdrängen von weißliberalem »small talk« – die triumphale Einsetzung einer schwarzen Regierung verlangt nach kräftigeren Farben und Tönen, einer Mischung aus Wunschdenken, Fakten und Fiktionen. Wie in den meisten ihrer Bücher überkreuzen sich auch hier Politik und Sexualität, die Geschichte scheint sich an den Irrwegen menschlicher Gefühle zu orientieren, und die utopischen Visionen bekommen etwas fremdartig Mystisches, das die Wahrscheinlichkeit einer Herrschaft der Schwarzen nicht glaubwürdiger macht. Es ist, in einem allgemeinen Sinn, der Niedergang des Liberalismus, der Nadine Gordimer zu schaffen macht. In einem Land, dessen weiße Minderheitsregierung ihre Scheinreformen als liberal ausgeben kann, hat dieser Begriff seine erklärende Kraft verloren. Nadine Gordimer wird nicht müde, darauf hinzuweisen, daß die Schwarzen nicht von den Weißen akzeptiert und an der Regierung beteiligt werden wollen, sondern daß es ihnen allein darum geht, die dreihundertfünfzigjährige Herrschaft der Weißen zu beenden und mit jeder Art von Diskriminierung Schluß zu machen. Der literarische Weg der Nadine Gordimer hat, über Umwege und Zwischenstationen, ins bedingungslose Engagement geführt, zu jener Haltung, die sie einmal so umschrieben hat: »Ich weiß heute,

daß Schriftsteller etwas leisten können, was anderen nicht ohne weiteres möglich ist: den Menschen dabei helfen, sich besser zu verstehen und zu begreifen, daß sie mitverantwortlich dafür sind, in welcher Art von Gesellschaft sie leben.«[6]
Sinnfälliger, unverhüllter noch als in den Romanen kommt ihr Anliegen in den Kurzgeschichten zum Ausdruck. Das rasche Erfassen und Durchdringen sozialer Konstellationen, die blitzartige Beleuchtung von Menschen in Krisensituationen, der gezielte Einsatz von Stilmitteln in den kürzeren Bauformen des Erzählens – alles das kommt der nüchternen, rationalen Seite ihrer Begabung entgegen, und so hat sie denn auch immer wieder betont, daß ihre Geschichten eigentlich nicht der Kommentierung bedürften: »If the story itself does not succeed in conveying all the writer meant it should, neither explication nor afterthought can change this.«[7] – *Some Monday For Sure* stammt aus den frühen sechziger Jahren – kurz nachdem der Roman *A World of Strangers* in Südafrika verboten worden war – und gehört zu jenem Stadium ihrer Entwicklung, in dem sie ihre Umgebung vor allem durch die Augen der Schwarzen sah. Der Lastwagen mit Sprengstoff, der von schwarzen Untergrundkämpfern (die sich nach dieser Aktion in alle Winde zerstreuen) aufgebracht wird, hat gewiß symbolische Bedeutung. Dem Erzähler, einem ehemaligen Tankwart, fällt es schwer, sich genau an den Tag des Überfalls zu erinnern – es war »some Monday, for sure«. Diese Redewendung soll andeuten, wie schwierig es sein kann, Ereignisse aus der Vergangenheit festzunageln – sie gewinnt durch Nadine Gordimers Erzählkunst aber auch eine Bedeutung für die Zukunft: »Some perfectly ordinary day, for sure, black South Africans will free themselves and rule themselves«,[8] wie es in der Einleitung zu einer Kurzgeschichtensammlung von 1975 heißt. Nicht die Gewißheit des Sieges der Schwarzen wird hier verkündet, sondern die Gewißheit des

6 Dorothea Razumovsky, »Die Angst trägt viele Namen. Eine Schriftstellerin in Südafrika: N. Gordimer«, in: *Frankfurter Allgemeine Zeitung*, 29. August 1981, S. 26.
7 Nadine Gordimer, *Selected Stories*, Harmondsworth 1978, S. 9.
8 Nadine Gordimer, *No Place Like. Selected Stories*, London 1975, S. 12.

Aufstandes, der Revolution, die für alle Beteiligten Risiken und Gefahren mit sich bringt. Die Schwarzen, deren Integrität und moralische Überlegenheit aus der Erfahrung des Leidens kommt, müssen sich über ihre Ziele klar werden. (Dabei ergeben sich bemerkenswerte Unterschiede in den Reaktionen von Frauen und Männern: gegen die gewaltbestimmte Männerwelt setzt Nadine Gordimer das irrationale Symbol der von Frauen gezeichneten Figuren an einer Hüttenwand – Figuren, die selbst die rauhsten Männer beunruhigen.)
In diesen Geschichten wird eine Technik erprobt, die es ermöglicht, gleichsam die innere Landschaft eines Menschen zu erforschen – ein Verfahren, das offensichtlich von der Notwendigkeit diktiert ist, sich in Südafrika unentwegt verstellen zu müssen, Strategien des Betrugs zu beherrschen. Das Thema erzwingt seinen Stil, einen Stil, der mit Absicht weniger zur Sprache bringt, als gemeint ist, eine Ausdrucksweise, die sich mit großer Vorsicht auf gefährlichem Terrain bewegt. Diese Vorsicht führt bisweilen zur Vagheit, ja Doppeldeutigkeit, dann aber auch zu subtiler Ironie. Wie unterirdische Stollen graben sich lakonische Aussagen über Reaktionen und Verhaltensweisen ins Bewußtsein der Leser und unterminieren alle Klischeevorstellungen über Südafrika. In der Geschichte *Which New Era Would That Be?* zum Beispiel erweist sich das Ideal der Rassenintegration als fragwürdig. Jake Alexander, ein Halbweißer, träumt von einer weißen Frau, »one of those big, soft, European women with curly yellow hair, with very high-heeled shoes that made them shake softly when they walked, with a strong scent, like hot flowers« (S. 43). Die liberale, intellektuelle, schwarzhaarige Frau, die solche Träume auslöst, stößt auf verletzende Ironie, als sie sich weigert, eine Geschichte zu glauben, in der ein Weißer es ablehnt, mit dem Schwarzen, dem er zuvor einen Drink angeboten hat, eine Mahlzeit einzunehmen. Die Stoßrichtung der Moral- und Gesellschaftskritik ist hier noch bestimmt von jener humanistischen Philanthropie, wie man sie aus der Zeit der Sklavenbefreiung in Amerika kennt; erst später kommt die Haltung eines auf politische Unabhängigkeit dringenden revolutionären Bewußtseins hinzu, eine Einstellung,

die mit den radikalen Reformbewegungen in der schwarzen Bevölkerung einhergeht. Skepsis gegenüber jenem penetranten Wohlwollen, das sich als aufgeklärte Menschenfreundlichkeit ausgibt, artikuliert sich nun in Erzählungen von Schwarzen, die aus blankem Opportunismus die von Weißen gebotenen Chancen annehmen, und von Weißen, deren behäbige Herablassung abstoßend wirkt.

Nadine Gordimer hat sich immer wieder mit Einstellungen auseinandergesetzt, die mit dem Begriff »Liberalismus« nur ungenau umschrieben sind. Die Weißen in *Town and Country Lovers* vertreten, wenn auch auf unterschiedliche Weise, Wertvorstellungen, die letztlich der englischen Tradition entstammen; sie spüren, daß die Traditionen und Moralbegriffe, an die sie sich klammern, in diesem Umfeld bedeutungslos geworden sind. Der europäische Wissenschaftler ebenso wie der südafrikanische Farmerssohn müssen erfahren, wie der intime Kontakt mit Menschen der anderen Hautfarbe zwangsläufig in die Tragödie führt; sie vertreten eine Zivilisation, deren Hilflosigkeit in Augenblicken der Belastung grotesk wirkt. Diese Menschen sind zutiefst verunsichert, weil der Staat selbst über die privatesten Momente Rechenschaft zu verlangen sich das Recht nimmt. Niemand kann sich geschützt fühlen, und noch die unschuldigste Beziehung nimmt vor diesem Hintergrund Züge des Beschmutzten an. Die berüchtigten südafrikanischen Gesetze über das Verbot sexueller Beziehungen zwischen Schwarzen und Weißen enthalten eine Definition der individuellen Freiheit in diesem Staat, wie sie entlarvender nicht sein kann. Nadine Gordimers fiktive Figuren leben in einer Atmosphäre der Bespitzelung und des Verrats, die sich bis ins Intimste erstreckt: auf nichts und niemanden ist Verlaß, und jedes Verhältnis wird zu einer Mischung aus Vergehen und Obstruktion.

Diese Schriftstellerin ist keine bloße Chronistin der Ereignisse in Südafrika; sie weigert sich beharrlich, die Rolle der im sicheren Exil lebenden, distanzierten Kommentatorin zu übernehmen. Ihre Ansichten über Südafrika und die Perspektiven ihres Erzählens von diesem Land haben sich mehrfach geändert. Anders als die meisten weißen südafrikanischen Schriftsteller versteht sie die Situation ihrer Heimat nicht als ein mit europäischen Maßstäben begreifbares Phänomen, sondern als eine neue, post-koloniale Wirklichkeit, die ihre eigenen Gesetze hat. »In diesem Land will ich leben«, sagt sie, »als Afrikanerin unter Afrikanern.«[9]

Helmut Winter

9 *Dialog* (s. Anm. 4).

Inhalt